Best Shade Plants

Stefan Buczacki
Best Shade Plants

HAMLYN

Executive Art Editor Robin Whitecross
Executive Editor Anna Mumford
Designer Michael Whitehead
Editor Selina Higgins
Production Alison Myer
Picture Research Emily Hedges

First published in Great Britain in 1994
by Hamlyn an imprint of Reed Consumer Books Limited
Michelin House, 81 Fulham Road, London SW3 6RB
and Auckland, Melbourne, Singapore and Toronto

Reprinted 1996

Produced by Mandarin Offset
Printed and bound in China

ISBN 0 600 57734 1

A catalogue of this book is available at the British Library

CONTENTS

INTRODUCTION

I well remember an old, very experienced and plain-speaking gardening friend's response to someone who once asked him how to cope with the problems of a shady garden. 'Look here, young man,' he responded, 'don't talk to me about the problems of shade because I can tell you that if I didn't have a good deal of it in my own garden, I'd jolly well have to invent some.' And that was that. This message and philosophy has stayed with me since: shade isn't a problem, it's an asset. Indeed, so important is shade for the growing of certain types of plant that a shade bed is highly desirable in anyone's garden.

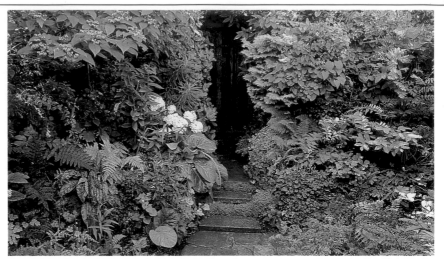

A truly verdant display of healthy and well-established shade plants

With few exceptions, there is no basic difference between a shade garden plant and a sun-lover. By and large, you can't tell them apart just by looking, and while there are some plant groups that do contain a high proportion of shade plants, most are an unpredictable mix of shade- and sun-loving species. Put on the spot, I would have to admit there are far more plants that could be grown in a shade garden than I have been able to include, but I have used a few reasoned criteria in making my selection.

I have chosen plants that have worked for me in shaded gardens and shaded beds of many different types and also those that I like and would commend to you on both aesthetic and horticultural grounds, wherever they happened to prefer growing. And I have included rather a high proportion of plants that positively demand shade, as well as some that merely tolerate it. In order to try to cater for those people whose gardens are completely shaded but who, nonetheless, want to try a little of everything, I have included representatives of most of the garden plant categories – bulbs, rock plants, climbers, shrubs, herbaceous perennials, ferns, annuals and grasses.

Whereas most sunny beds and borders rely heavily on flowers for their colour and attractiveness, it must be accepted that in the shade garden this will generally almost always be less true. Flowering plants that are adapted to grow only in shade must produce flowers in order to perpetuate themselves, but these flowers are quite commonly less dramatic and less brightly coloured than those of the open garden. And those plants that I have described as shade tolerant, as opposed to shade demanding, will very often flower less effectively, if at all, when grown in shade, their appeal coming instead from their foliage or overall form.

Many shrubs find their natural home in woodland, as do many herbaceous perennials, and it is no coincidence that these constitute the biggest sections in the book. Ferns are very well represented but ornamental grasses are few in number and rock plants even more so. The rock plant is, by and large, a plant of sunny, exposed places, and there are relatively few, usually those that live in crevices, that can grow in shade. Bulbs are fairly well represented, and include types that grow naturally in deciduous woodland and are able to flower early, before the tree canopy expands making the habitat much darker. Few annuals are included because the ability to grow and flower quickly in low light levels hasn't been mastered by many of them. The familiar group of water plants is absent totally; it just isn't possible to produce a garden pool in shade.

What I really hope to convey, however, is the notion that gardening in the shade is no harder, no less rewarding, no more restricting and certainly no less enjoyable than gardening with any other environmental constraint.

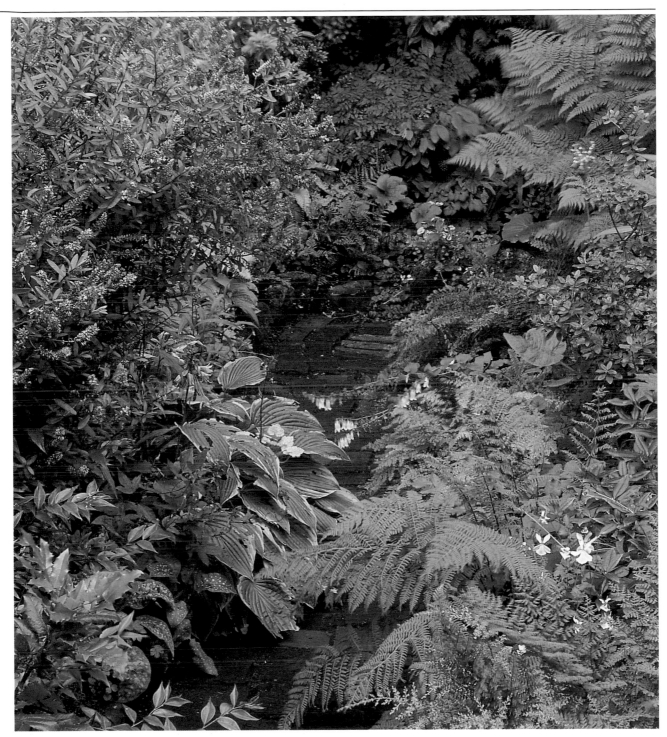

A decorative corner of a richly planted shade garden

THE SCIENCE OF SHADE

All of the plants in this book and all of the plants that grow in our gardens are basically green. Those with purple leaves are green 'underneath' and even those with yellow leaves have other parts that are green. This green colour in plants is due to the presence of a chemical pigment called chlorophyll which is sometimes masked by pigments of other colours.

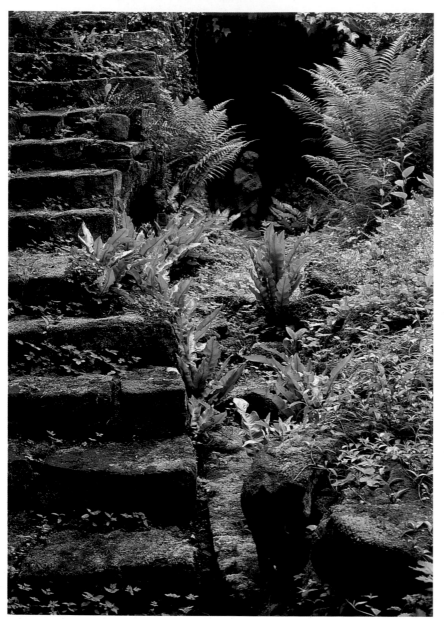

Ferns are good examples of plants than can grow in very low light levels

Chlorophyll is not present in animals, nor in fungi, but occurs in algae, all flowering plants, in ferns and their relatives. Arguably the most important chemical on our planet, it confers on those organisms possessing it an ability to use sunlight to manufacture essential food stuffs from the raw materials of carbon dioxide and water. The chlorophyll can be thought of as the catalyst for the chemical reactions to take place, the whole process being called photosynthesis. In the shaded garden the vital ingredient of sunlight is of course in very short supply.

HOW PLANTS MANAGE
TO GROW IN SHADE

Shade plants have developed systems that make optimum use of the sunlight that *does* reach a shaded area; for no green plants will grow in the complete dark or in extremely low light levels, although ferns will do their best. Ferns are probably among the more extreme. Many people will have seen them growing perfectly satisfactorily in really very gloomy conditions such as in caves and on the internal walls of wells, but the way that they can make do with so little light is a bit mysterious.

In many instances, we can see simply by looking at the structure of the leaf that it has adapted in order to capture as much light as possible. Some plants in shaded places (and, again, many ferns are good examples) have broad, flattened leaves, angled so as to receive as much sunlight as possible. And when these leaves are examined microscopically, they will be seen to have very thin surface cell layers so that light can penetrate readily to the chorophyll-containing cells which, in turn, are usually sited close to the surface.

This might imply that, merely by looking at a plant, it is possible to determine if it would be a good subject for a shady place, but there are so many variations and clearly so many different mechanisms within plants that relate to shade tolerance that it would be dangerous to rely fully on mere observation. From what I have said about the importance of chlorophyll, however, it should be evident that a leaf that is deficient in chlorophyll will have a problem in a low-light area. And so it is. Plants with variegated leaves have the leaf chlorophyll confined to certain areas, with yellow or other coloured pigments showing through in the remainder. What is a useful maxim, therefore, is that plants with variegated leaves generally tend to be slower growing and less vigorous overall in the shade than their all-green counterparts; and some will adapt to being grown in a shady place by losing their variegation and becoming all green. Some variegated ivies display this phenomenon very noticeably and 'revert' to green if grown in shade. Plants that combine variegated foliage and shade tolerance are less frequently encountered and, therefore, more to be prized. Plants with purple or reddish leaves seem to have less of a problem because the chlorophyll isn't lacking, merely masked to our eyes by another pigment.

THE IMPORTANCE OF MOISTURE

Leaves aren't designed only for photosynthesis; it is through leaves that water is lost to the atmosphere, to be replaced by water drawn up the plant from the roots and the soil. A leaf that is adapted, with flattened, broad leaves, to receive the optimum amount of sun-

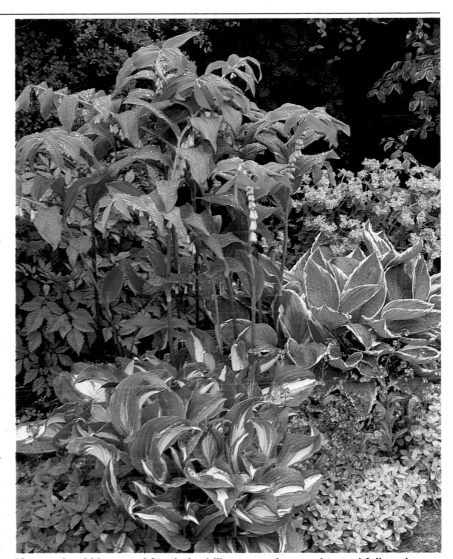

Hostas should be noted for their ability to produce variegated foliage in a shady position. Both *Alchemilla* and *Hosta* are very useful as ground cover

light will also inevitably present an ideal surface for water evaporation and loss. This could lead to the problem of too much water loss but, fortunately, shady places are often damp, and with a moisture-laden atmosphere around the plant, evaporation will be lessened and so in this case no difficulty arises. The real problem occurs with those places that are not only shady but warm and dry, too, for this truly presents a leaf with a conundrum in trying to capture sunlight while still retaining enough moisture to be able to grow satisfactorily. Nature being what it is, some plants have adapted even to this dilemma, but the practical consequence is that plants that will thrive in dry shaded places are distinctly few in number and are, therefore, to be treasured.

TYPES OF SHADE

It might be imagined that a shady garden is a shady garden, and that it matters little how the shade is produced. But in reality, there are important differences from one site to another, and while I would never suggest that a particular gardener had 'the wrong kind of shade', I would urge a little thought before planting.

Intensity of shade varies considerably and in the accounts of individual plants, I have indicated whether they will tolerate light, medium or deep shade in the hope that most people will understand roughly what I have in mind. My intent is perhaps best envisaged by imagining a walk from the very edge of a wood, where the shade is light, beneath the first trees, where it will be moderate, and finally to the centre of the wood where it will be deep.

But these degrees of shade could also be realized by having an area of a garden that is shaded for only part of the day. In these situations, shade for perhaps half the morning would constitute light shade, shade for half the day moderate shade and shade for almost the whole day, deep shade. To specify the difference between my garden and woodland examples, I have referred sometimes to dappled shade, to indicate that some plants are less likely to be successful where the changing angle of the sun, rather than the intervening tree canopy, is responsible for the effect. But I should also stress that there is no absolute rule and my comments are derived purely from personal experience. No one has deliberately grown each plant under a defined light regime and measured the

Some species of *Campanula* grow very successfully in light, dappled shade

intensity like a cricket umpire, so it will often be worth experimentation where your conditions are at least close to those I recommend.

DEEPEST YEAR-ROUND SHADE

This is to be expected beneath evergreen trees, especially conifers (trying to grow plants beneath yew can be like gardening at night), although while they are in leaf some deciduous species, such as beech, can be almost equally shade casting. Walls will usually produce a deeper shade than hedges or fences (which often allow at least some light to pass through, making for a dappled effect) and common sense suggests that the higher the wall the greater the duration of the shade. A bed adjoining the wall on the darkest side of a house, for instance, may receive almost no direct sunlight at all.

HEAT IN THE SHADE

Light is generally associated with heat, and just as a sunny position is a warm one, so a shaded position will be cooler. But the shadiest position need not necessarily be the place for the most hardy of your plants. As I have indicated, a fully-shaded aspect will generally be overall the coldest part of your garden and it will receive the least sun. But in winter, this may be no bad thing, for the damage caused to plants by winter cold results rather more from the rapidity with which their frozen tissues thaw than from the absolute minimum temperature. So, in reality, plants growing in a less shaded aspect but where they will be at risk of being struck by the early morning sunshine and so thawing out quickly, are likely to suffer more damage than those in a darker one.

PLANTS AND PLANTING

Most perennials for your shade garden are likely to be bought rather than raised from seed and most of these, (certainly the more common ones) will be in containers and so can be planted out at any time of the year. Less common and larger plants bought by mail order are more likely to be delivered during the dormant winter period, bare-rooted or perhaps root-balled (fairly loosely packed in organic matter contained within a plastic bag or similar container). A bare-rooted or root balled plant should either be put promptly into its growing position, or be heeled in temporarily by digging a fairly shallow hole and covering the roots with soil.

PREPARING A PERMANENT PLANTING POSITION

This should be prepared by digging a hole of roughly twice the volume of the pot ball of compost, if the plant is in a container, or twice the root spread of one that is bare-rooted or root balled. The soil removed should be mixed with a roughly equal volume of compost or similar organic matter plus a few handfuls of bone meal. This is rich in phosphate which aids root development and will help the plant to establish quickly.

PLANTING BARE-ROOTED AND CONTAINER-GROWN PLANTS

The roots should be spread carefully in the planting hole and any that are damaged, wayward or crossing, cut off. Gently replace the soil and compost mixture in the hole, moving the plant up and down, if necessary, to ensure

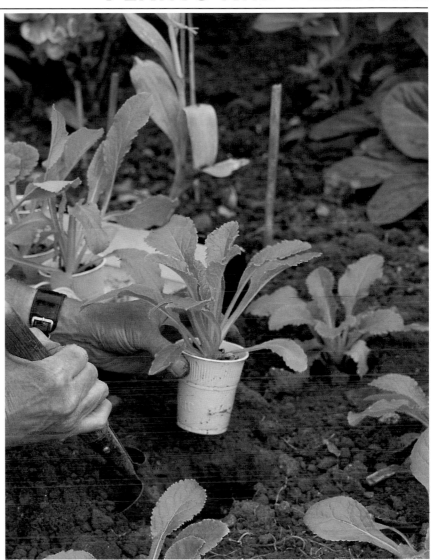

Planting out *Campanula* (Canterbury Bells)

that no air pockets remain among the roots. I prefer to tease away the roots lightly around the edge of the compost ball of a container-grown plant otherwise they tend to grow inwards, towards the generally more moist compost in the centre rather than out into the surrounding soil. Firm the soil carefully with your boot as you fill the hole but don't ram it down too hard. And finally, finish by making a small mound with the soil sloping away from the plant's stem to prevent water from collecting at the base, freezing and causing damage. Water the plant well after planting, stake it, if necessary, and keep the area immediately around its base free from weeds and other vegetation.

FOOD AND WATER

Food and water are, of course, important for all garden plants. The argument that plants growing in the wild manage without our intervention and that applying fertilizer is wasted effort cuts little ice with me, for the wild plant is generally a poor performer when set alongside its cultivated counterpart. The varieties bred or selected for garden use invariably have bigger or otherwise better flowers, lusher foliage and generally greater vigour, all of which must be satisfied by correspondingly more nutrient. And generally speaking, the smaller and shorter lived the individual plant, the more will a shortage of fertilizer become significant.

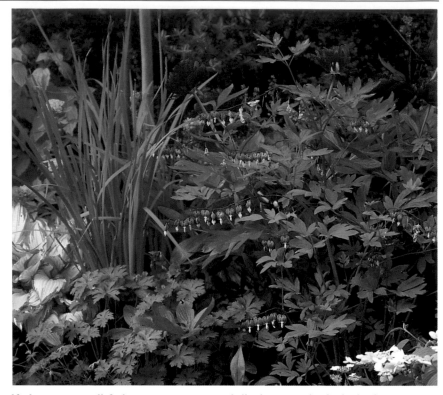

If plants are well-fed you can get a good display even in dark shade

IMPORTANCE OF FERTILIZERS

Shady conditions tend to magnify the difference that using a fertilizer can make, especially for those plants that are merely shade tolerant. For shade creates what gardeners call a marginal situation: the plants are growing in less than optimal conditions and the balance is best tipped in their favour by regular and sensible supplementary feeding. The most useful general purpose fertilizer is one containing more or less equal parts of nitrogen (N), phosphate (P) and potassium (K), and I find that fish, blood and bone with an N:P:K: ratio of around 5:5:6 gives excellent results. However, others are available; the artificially based Growmore, for instance, has a 7:7:7 ratio. For most purposes, a small handful, (about 70g per square metre (2oz per yd) should

be applied in spring, although I have indicated in the text any exceptions to this general rule.

I have indicated that some plants may be reluctant to flower in the shade and a fertilizer with a slightly higher content of potassium, such as most proprietary rose fertilizers, will be beneficial. Alternatively, the general balanced fertilizer dose could be supplemented with a quarter as much again of potassium sulphate. Particularly fast growing plants (this applies especially to climbers), may additionally be given a balanced liquid fertilizer on a one or two weekly basis during the growing season.

IMPORTANCE OF MULCHES

Water is important, too, and although the shade garden can often be damp, in

situations where there is shelter from drying sun and wind, it may, on the contrary, sometimes be very dry, as for instance when the shade is provided by a wall, fence or hedge. So while applying a mulch in the early part of the year when the soil is still damp is important in any shade garden, it is vitally important in a naturally dry one, where it may make the difference between genuine success and the plants barely managing to produce anything that is worthwhile. Almost any normal organic mulching material can be used but where shade is provided by large shrubs or trees, compost or leaf mould provides much the best material and will, of course, contribute a small but nevertheless important amount of nutrient also.

SOIL

Shade has no direct effect on the basic nature of soil, but a soil that is permanently shaded may have a number of differences from one that is in full sun. All soils are the same in their essential make-up of sand, silt, clay and humus, and it is the relative proportions of each of these components that give each soil type its own characteristic features.

A soil that has a high clay content will be slow to warm up in the early part of the year, but will then retain warmth well and is also likely to have a fairly high nutrient content. A light, sandy soil, by contrast, will be relatively low in nutrients, and will warm up quickly but also lose heat and cool down quickly, too. In dry conditions, such as against a shady wall, a clay soil can become hard and impenetrable whereas, in wet conditions, it may be waterlogged. So while a clay soil is potentially a better garden soil, it is much more difficult to manage in its unaltered state.

HUMUS

Humus, which is simply the part-decomposed remains of plants, will improve both sandy and clay soils because it contains natural gel-like substances that bind together the soil particles to improve the crumb structure and, more importantly, the ratio between crumbs and pores through which air and water can move; the balance, if you like, between solid matter and holes. It is very important, therefore, to dig in organic matter to any soil; annually if the plants are to be changed annually, or before planting if the plants are to be longer-term propositions. But even in a long-term planting, adding more organic matter to the surface of the soil each year in the form of mulch is very important, not only for the reasons that I outline on p. 12 but also because it will slowly be taken down into the body of the soil through the action of earthworms.

ACIDITY AND ALKALINITY

Apart from the physical ingredients of the soil, there is one other matter of importance that will affect the choice of plants: its relative acidity or alkalinity. An acid soil is one with a pH below 7, an alkaline soil, one with a pH above 7, pH 7 being known as neutral. Most garden plants thrive best in soils around pH 6.5, just on the acidic side of neutral, but there are exceptions. And in a shade garden, the most important exceptions are rhododendrons and azaleas, lovely classic woodland shrubs but which must have a truly acid soil, ideally with a pH below 5. If you don't already have an acid soil, you mustn't be tempted by such horticultural delights, for it is simply not feasible to lower the pH significantly. If, conversely, you have a moderately acidic soil, you can raise the pH, which will enable you to grow those plants which require more neutral conditions, simply by adding lime. The amount of lime to add will vary with the soil type and initial pH, but any carton of garden lime that you buy should tell you how to calculate the dose for different soils.

Rhododendrons need both acidic soil and shade in order to thrive

PESTS AND DISEASES

All garden plants are liable to be attacked by pests and diseases and those growing in the shade are likely to be affected more by some and less by others. But the same overall principles apply: prevention is better than cure, but there are limits to how reliable this can be. There are chemical and non-chemical ways of combating problems, not always of equal effectiveness, and the decision on how important a particular problem is and how much damage is tolerable is very much a personal one.

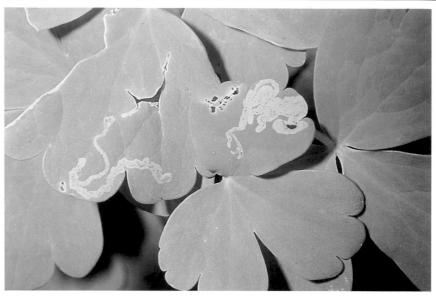

Aquilegia **leaf miner**

PESTS

These are members of the animal kingdom that cause damage to plants, and in shaded beds fairly remote from buildings, such as plantings beneath trees, the larger types (mammals such as voles, rabbits and deer) may be disproportionately important. Nonetheless, the biggest problems are still likely to come from small pests – especially insects of many types and also some mites. All, of course, are cold-blooded and so their activity and reproductive rate increase in warm weather. Insect pests can be divided roughly into two groups: the sap-sucking types, such as aphids, whiteflies and scale insects, that achieve much of their impact through force of numbers, gradually wearing down a plant's vigour; and the chewing types, such as caterpillars and beetles, that may be small in quantity but are rather large in effect for they remove pieces of the plant bodily.

DISEASES

These are caused most importantly by microscopic fungi: the mildews and rusts that I illustrate on page 16 are familiar examples and, by and large, they thrive in sheltered conditions. All fungi require moisture for their spores to germinate and grow but, contrary to what is sometimes thought, not all require damp conditions thereafter, the most important exception being the type called powdery mildews. These are the most important plant-attacking mildew fungi, and after their initial germination they then thrive best in hot dry conditions. Thus, the diseases likely to occur in dry shade may be somewhat different from those that occur in more moist conditions.

Viruses A few plant diseases are caused by viruses, usually introduced by aphids or other sap-sucking pests. The effects are much more indefinite than those of fungal diseases and usually take the form of crinkling or crumpling of the leaves, indefinite leaf mottling and sometimes overall feeble growth. However, it usually requires an expert to distinguish between these effects and those arising from other causes, such as inadequate feeding.

SOLUTIONS

Given this information about how pests and diseases thrive, what can be done to minimise their effects? The ideal would be to choose types and varieties of plant that have natural resistance to them but, in practice, this is very rarely feasible. Unlike the situation with food crops, no one has much bothered to go to either the trouble or the expense of breeding varieties of ornamental plants with this in mind.

A second approach is to create an environment less attractive to the pests and diseases, but this is also difficult because discouraging one may in turn encourage another. The third line of defence is to keep an eye open for the initial signs of attack early in the season and then to physically nip off the problem. Certainly, pinching out small aphid colonies or the shoot-tips carrying the

SYMPTOMS ON LEAVES

PROBLEM	DETAIL	PROBABLE CAUSE
Wilting	General	Shortage of water Root pest, or disease Wilt disease
Holed	Generally ragged	Small pests (millepedes, woodlice) Capsid bugs
	Elongate holes; usually with slime present	Slugs or snails
	Fairly large holes over entire leaf or confined to edges	Caterpillars, beetles
Discoloured	Black	Sooty mould
	Predominantly red	Shortage of water
	More or less bleached	Fertilizer deficiency Shortage of water Too much water
	Irregular yellowish patterns	Virus
	Irregular tunnels	Leaf miners
	Surface flecking	Leaf hoppers
	Brown (scorched) in spring	Frost
Spotted	Brownish, irregular, no mould	Leaf spot
	Small, dusty, brown, black or bright yellow-orange-coloured	Rust
Mouldy	Black	Sooty mould
	Grey, fluffy	Grey mould
	White, (or rarely brown), velvety	Mildew
Infested with insects	White, tiny, moth-like	Whiteflies
	Green, grey, black or other colour	Aphids
	Flat, encrusted, like limpets	Scale insects
	Large, six legs, worm-like	Caterpillars
Cobwebs present	Leaves also discoloured	Red spider mites

SYMPTOMS ON FLOWERS

PROBLEM	DETAIL	PROBABLE CAUSE
Drooping	General	Shortage of water End of flowering period
Tattered	Masses of tiny holes	Caterpillars
	Large pieces torn away	Birds
Removed entirely	Usually discarded nearby	Birds
Discoloured	Powdery white covering	Mildew
Mouldy	Fluffy grey mould	Grey mould (*Botrytis*)

SYMPTOMS ON STEMS OR BRANCHES

PROBLEM	DETAIL	PROBABLE CAUSE
Eaten through	On young plants	Slugs or snails
	On older plants	Mice, voles, rabbits
Infested with insects	Green, grey, black or other colour	Aphids
	Flat, encrusted, like limpets	Scale insects
	Large, six legs, worm-like	Caterpillars
Rotten	At base, young plants	Stem and foot rot
	On woody climbers	Decay fungus
Blister on woody stems	More or less spherical	Gall
	Target-like	Canker
Dying back	General	Shortage of water Canker, or coral spot Root pest, or disease

PESTS AND DISEASES

Mahonia rust

No gardener these days can fail to appreciate that over-use of chemicals in the garden will cause harm to the environment. Very few chemicals can discriminate between good and harmful insects, some have unfortunate side-effects on other organisms (some insecticides, for example, are harmful to fish) and yet others may persist in the soil with rather uncertain long-term consequences. And I must emphasise that these effects are at least as likely to be brought about by so-called natural or organic products as they are by artificial ones. My advice, therefore, is only to use chemicals in moderation, to use them as the last rather than the first option, and to use them only in the manner and at the doses that the manufacturers indicate.

I have listed the most common and important garden fungicides and insec-

first tell-tale whitening of mildew in the spring will delay the onset of serious damage, and is to be encouraged. But it will only occasionally be the complete answer and it is then that more direct action is needed, and personal choice becomes important.

ticides and also given a key to the most frequent problems likely to be found on shade-garden plants, with my suggested treatments. For convenience, I've also included symptoms of the very few instances of fertilizer deficiency that are likely to be encountered.

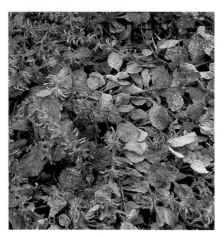

Mildew on *Ajuga*

SOME FUNGICIDES, INSECTICIDES AND PESTICIDAL CHEMICALS USEFUL FOR CONTROLLING PROBLEMS ON SHADE PLANTS

FUNGICIDES	USES AND COMMENTS
Benomyl Carbendazim Thiophanate-methyl	Systemic•, for most foliage and stem diseases, including mildew and grey mould
Myclobutanil	Systemic, especially useful for leaf spots and rust
Propiconazole	Systemic, especially useful for leaf spots and rust
Triforine	Systemic, many foliage diseases
Sulphur*	Non-systemic, many foliage diseases

SLUG AND SNAIL KILLERS	USES AND COMMENTS
Methiocarb	As pellets
Metaldehyde	As pellets, mini-pellets or liquid

INSECTICIDES	USES AND COMMENTS
Dimethoate	Systemic, most pests
Derris*	Contact, most pests
Natural soaps*	Contact, most pests
Permethrin	Contact, most pests
Phoxim	Contact, soil pests
Pirimicarb	Contact, specific to aphids
Pyrethrum*	Contact, most pests
Tar oil	Contact

Note: It should be noted that some of these chemicals are only available in particular formulations or in combination with certain other chemicals. Some may also be marketed for specific pest or disease problems only. In every case, you must read the label directions carefully to be sure that the product is being used for the purpose and in the manner for which it is intended. The names given above are those of the active chemical ingredients. These will not be the same as the product names but will be found printed on the product label.

* Generally acceptable to organic gardeners

• Systemic substances are absorbed by the plant and so require less frequent and less accurate spraying than contact materials.

TREATMENTS FOR COMMON PEST AND DISEASE PROBLEMS ON SHADE PLANTS

PROBLEM	TREATMENT	PROBLEM	TREATMENT
Aphids	Use any proprietary contact insecticide; pick off affected shoots by hand or wash insects off with hose.	Millepedes	Dust affected area with derris.
Beetles	Normally, treatment is not necessary or justified but in cases of extensive attack use any proprietary contact insecticide.	Rabbits	The only sure protection is to use a wire netting fence with the lower edge turned outwards at 90° over the soil surface.
Birds	Erect netting or other protection; in really severe cases, erect bird scarers but remember that all birds enjoy legal protection and may not be harmed.	Red spider mites	No treatment is really feasible, although keeping plants well watered and mulched will help limit the impact of attacks.
Canker	Cut out and destroy affected branches; no chemical treatment is possible.	Root pests	Normally, no treatment is feasible but, with severe and persistent attacks, dust around affected plants with derris or other soil insecticide.
Capsid bugs	The insects are too unpredictable and erratic in occurrence to make any treatment feasible.	Root disease	Destroy severely affected plants.
Caterpillars	Pick off by hand if the caterpillars can be found and are present in small numbers. If masses of insects occur, pick off and destroy entire affected leaves or use any proprietary contact insecticide.	Rust	Spray with propiconazole fungicide.
		Scale insects	Spray or drench with systemic insecticide.
Coral spot	Cut away and destroy affected branches or twigs, cutting well into the healthy wood. On valuable ornamental plants, spray the surrounding branches with a systemic fungicide.	Slugs	Use proprietary slug pellets or liquid controls, or home-made remedies such as traps baited with beer. Surround the base of plants with fine powders, such as ash or soot, or a low barrier of finely spiny twigs such as gorse.
Fertilizer deficiency	Give liquid fertilizer (see p. 12).	Snails	If serious, use methods recommended for slugs but generally snails are less serious, fewer in number and can be combated by collecting them by hand and by locating and eradicating them from their hiding places.
Fungal decay	Destroy affected parts; no other treatment is feasible.		
Gall	Normally no treatment is justified, but cut out if severely disfiguring.		
Grey mould	Destroy affected parts; spray with systemic fungicide.	Sooty mould	Wash off mould with water or destroy badly affected leaves and then identify and treat the insect pest responsible for forming the honeydew on which the mould grows.
Leaf hoppers	The insects are too erratic and unpredictable to make any treatment practicable.	Stem and foot rot	Little can be done but, as it is often associated with waterlogging, improve drainage of the affected area.
Leaf miners	Remove and destroy affected leaves on herbaceous plants.	Virus	Effects are usually mild, so no treatment is necessary.
Leaf spot	In most instances no treatment is necessary, for leaf spot diseases are rarely severe. Where attacks appear to be related to general poor growth, however, spray with systemic fungicide.	Voles	Set mouse traps or use proprietary poison baits.
		Whiteflies	No treatment is feasible on outdoor plants.
Mice	Set traps or use proprietary poison baits.	Wilt disease	Drench around plants with systemic fungicide.
Mildew	Ensure that plants are not allowed to become too dry and apply systemic fungicide or sulphur.	Woodlice	Dust around plants with soil insecticide.

BULBS

Anemone

> *What a big and varied genus this is, and fairly shade tolerant, on the whole, with some of the herbaceous types appearing elsewhere in the book. But the little tuber- and rhizome-forming species will always be highest in my affections. Among them is one of the most delightful native European plants, the wood anemone,* Anemone nemorosa, *white flowered in the wild form although with coloured variants, but there are related species from both Europe and Asia, most notably the exquisite sky-blue* A. blanda. *"*

Anemone nemorosa 'Alba Plena'

SHADE TOLERANCE Light, dappled shade under deciduous trees; I find that *A. nemorosa* is more tolerant than other species.
SOIL Well-drained, humus-rich is best for *A. nemorosa* but lighter, more free-draining soils are tolerated by the others. Drought tolerant when dormant.
HARDINESS Very hardy, tolerating -25°C (-13°F).
SIZE 10cm (4in) unless stated otherwise.

PLANTING
As tubers or rhizomes, 3-4cm (1-1½in) deep. *A. nemorosa* can be difficult to start into growth in the open ground and it may be wiser to plant the tubers in small pots of soil-based potting compost and then plant out when in full leaf.

CARE
Apply a light dressing of general-purpose or bulb fertilizer in spring. Don't disturb, if possible, once established.

PROPAGATION
By division of tuber clumps; most are very variable from seed.

PROBLEMS
None.

RECOMMENDED VARIETIES

Anemone nemorosa spring-flowering, normal species is pure white, single and exquisite, but among the best of many varieties are 'Alba Plena' double white, 'Robinsoniana' pale lavender, and 'Royal Blue' deep blue; *A. apennina* spring-flowering, variable, white, pink or blue; *A. blanda* early-spring-flowering, normal species is variable in colour and the best form is called simply 'Blue' but other good varieties are 'Ingramii' (also called 'Atrocaerulea') deep blue, 'Pink Star' pale pink and 'Radar' magenta with white centre; *A. ranunculoides* spring-flowering, yellow, 20cm (8in).

Arisarum

> *The arum family is a predominantly tropical group and it comes as a surprise to many gardeners, to discover that the exotic-looking mouse plant,* Arisarum proboscideum, *is a temperate species from southern Europe. Its brown or dark purplish spathe which appears after the leaves in late spring and summer has a slender, tail-like extension and the whole combines to give the impression of a tiny rodent vanishing into its burrow. "*

SHADE TOLERANCE Light to moderate.
SOIL Moist but not waterlogged, humus-rich for *A. proboscideum*, drier for *A. vulgare*.
HARDINESS Fairly hardy, tolerating -5°C (23°F).
SIZE 10cm (4in).

Arisarum proboscideum

PLANTING
As rhizomes 15cm (6in) deep.
CARE
Little needed but a light dressing of general-purpose fertilizer may be given in spring. Disturb these rhizomes as little as possible once established.
PROPAGATION
By division of rhizomes when dormant, or by seed using the half-hardy technique in spring or autumn.
PROBLEMS
None.

RECOMMENDED VARIETIES
True species only available. The related *Arisarum vulgare* flowers early in the year and has attractive dark and light stripes on the spathe but lacks the tail-like extension of *A. proboscideum*.

Arum

❝ *There's no more typical member of the arum family than Arum itself and many people will have delighted in the native cuckoo pint or lords and ladies,* Arum maculatum, *with its fresh leaves in winter, the greenish spathe in early summer and the vivid red fruiting spike in autumn. I find it a useful-enough plant in my woodland garden, but even prettier are its relatives,* A. italicum *and* A. creticum, *especially the marbled-leaf variety of the former. Its leaves are often used by flower arrangers, as indeed are the fruiting spikes, although it's perhaps worth noting that the fruits themselves are poisonous.* ❞

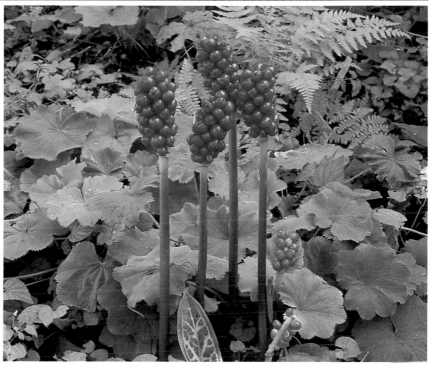
Arum italicum

PLANTING
As plants, up to the soil mark on the stem base or as dormant tubers 10-15cm (4-6in) deep.
CARE
Little needed once established, but a light dressing of general-purpose fertilizer may be given in spring. Avoid disturbing if possible. The fruits are commonly eaten by slugs and it may then be worth removing the damaged fruiting spike.
PROPAGATION
By careful division of plants in spring or autumn, or by seed: collect fresh, ripe fruits and thoroughly wash away the fleshy covering, sow in humus-rich soil-based compost at about 20°C (68°F). Germination is slow.
PROBLEMS
None.

SHADE TOLERANCE
Moderate to deep.
SOIL Moist but not waterlogged, humus-rich.
HARDINESS Fairly hardy (*A. creticum*) to hardy (*A. maculatum*) tolerating -5 to -15°C (23-5°F).
SIZE (spathe) Up to 20-25cm (8-10in).

RECOMMENDED VARIETIES
True species only usually available of *Arum maculatum*. The best form of *A. italicum* is usually called 'Pictum' but can also be known as *A. i. marmoratum* or *A. i. italicum*. The yellow-spathed *A. creticum* can sometimes be found in selected colour forms.

BULBS

Asarum Wild Ginger

❝ *Really attractive and striking evergreen shade-tolerant ground-cover plants aren't especially abundant, and so the various rhizomatous species of* Asarum *should be appreciated much more widely. The leaves are rich and glossy and often have pleasant spicy scents. The flowers are insignificant and usually hidden beneath the foliage which is no bad thing as their perfume is distinctly unappealing.* ❞

SHADE TOLERANCE
Moderate to deep.
SOIL Moist but not waterlogged, humus-rich.
HARDINESS Fairly hardy
(A. hartwegii) to hardy
(A. europaeum) tolerating -5 to -15°C (23-5°F).
SIZE 10cm (4in) tall, 25-30cm (10-12in) spread.

PLANTING
As plants, up to the soil mark on the stem base.

CARE
Little needed once established, but a

RECOMMENDED VARIETIES
The most commonly available species are the north American *Asarum caudatum* and European *A. europaeum*, both with heart- or kidney-shaped dark green leaves, and the North American *A. hartwegii*, with heart-shaped and attractively silver-marbled leaves.

light dressing of general-purpose fertilizer may be given in spring.

PROPAGATION
By careful division of plants in spring or autumn, or by seed, using the half-hardy technique with fresh seed in a soil-based compost.

PROBLEMS
Slugs.

Cardiocrinum

❝ *Cardiocrinum giganteum was once classed as a lily but, truly, no lily was ever this large and, with every justification, it now has a genus of its own. Well grown, it must be among the most spectacular of all woodland plants, but it needs a big garden and trees with high branches for it to be shown off properly. It is an oriental species of truly imposing proportions, with highly elongated, lily-like, white trumpet flowers with purple centres, that appear in summer.* ❞

PLANTING
As bulbs, with the tip just below soil level, unlike almost all true lilies which require deep planting.

CARE
Remove dead flower heads and cut

Asarum europaeum

Cardiocrinum giganteum

down old foliage once it has browned and shrivelled. Mulch with leaf mould in autumn and spring, and top dress lightly in spring, with bone meal. Don't disturb, if possible, once established.

PROPAGATION

By removal and replanting of daughter bulbs after flowering, or by seed sown shallowly in a soil-based, humus-rich compost at about 20°C (68°F).

RECOMMENDED VARIETIES

Usually, only the true species is available but the variety *Cardiocrinum giganteum yunnanense*, slightly shorter and with purple flowers, is sometimes offered.

SHADE TOLERANCE

Moderate, preferably dappled under deciduous trees.
SOIL Moist, deep, well-drained, rich in leaf mould and preferably not drying out even in summer.
HARDINESS Moderately hardy, tolerating -15°C (5°F) provided mulch protection is given.
SIZE Up to 4m (13ft) in ideal conditions, but 2m (6ft) should easily be attainable.

PROBLEMS

Slugs will eat young leaves and shoots, mice and voles may nibble the bulbs.

Chionodoxa
Glory of the snow

❝ This must be one of the easiest and obliging of all small spring-flowering bulbs, self-seeding more readily than any other bulb in my garden. I confess that I have never seen it adding glory to the snow, but apparently it does so in its native Turkish mountains. Its little electric-blue and white flowers will add appeal to any part of the garden and, although it isn't usually considered a shade plant, it grows so effectively for me in the lightly shaded area at the edge of a group of trees, decorating the bare ground with its tiny blue sapphires. ❞

PLANTING

As bulbs, with the base at a depth of about 4cm (1½in).

CARE

Little needed, since dead flowers and

foliage tend to shrivel away, but it is useful to top dress lightly in spring with bone meal.

PROPAGATION

By division of clumps and replanting of daughter bulbs or by the removal of the numerous self-sown seedlings that will be close by.

PROBLEMS

None.

SHADE TOLERANCE Light, preferably dappled.
SOIL Most, provided it is well-drained; tolerant of considerable dryness and drought tolerant when dormant.
HARDINESS Hardy, tolerating -20°C (-4°F).
SIZE Flower stalk up to about 12cm (5in).

RECOMMENDED VARIETIES

Although there are several species, the commonest and, I think, prettiest are *Chionodoxa luciliae* and its larger-flowered and slightly taller form, often called *C. gigantea*. I have no experience of the shade tolerance of the others.

BULBS

Colchicum
Autumn crocus,
Naked ladies

❝ These are impressive and attractive but frustratingly tricky bulbs, the trickiness arising because of their nakedness. They obtain their common name from the habit of the goblet-shaped flowers which appear on tall bare stems before the leaves emerge, and these stems are fragile, so the large flowers are apt to flop over with rain and wind. My solutions are either to grow them among taller vegetation such as grass, which provides some support, or to place them some-where very sheltered. ❞

PLANTING
As corms, with the base at a depth of about 15cm (6in).
CARE
Little needed, but it is advantageous to mulch in autumn, and top dress lightly in spring with bone meal.
PROPAGATION
Best by the division of clumps and

SHADE TOLERANCE Light, preferably dappled.
SOIL Most, provided it is well-drained and fairly rich in humus.
HARDINESS Hardy to very hardy, tolerating at least -20°C (-4°F), although other species are more tender.
SIZE Flower stalk up to about 15cm (6in).

replanting of daughter corms, or alternatively by sowing fresh seed in a soil-based compost at about 20°C (68°F); germination tends to be slow. Named varieties generally do not come true from seed.
PROBLEMS
Slugs.

RECOMMENDED VARIETIES
Although there are many species and varieties, I find the slightly smaller-flowered species better than the larger, selected varieties for growing in shade. Among the best and most widely available are the purple-pink-flowered *Colchicum autumnale* and the more deeply purple *C. speciosum*.

Convallaria
Lily-of-the-valley

❝ There never was a more loved and characteristic cottage garden plant than the sweetly scented, white bell-flowered lily-of-the-valley, Convallaria majalis. *I am deeply fond of its delicate spring blooms and tough, strap-like, ground-covering foliage, but am aware that it does have its detractors because, once entrenched, it can become invasive and in a small garden will take on an almost weed-like stubbornness. Paradoxically, other gardeners find it difficult to establish at all, so there must be some elusive soil characteristic that it requires. ❞*

SHADE TOLERANCE
Moderate to deep but it flowers better when only moderate.
SOIL Most, provided it is well-drained and fairly rich in humus, but see my remarks on establishing above.
HARDINESS Very hardy, tolerating at least -20°C (-4°F).
SIZE Flower stalk up to about 20cm (8in).

PLANTING
As plants in full leaf or as rhizomes, about 7-8cm (2½-3in) deep.
CARE
Little needed, but it is advantageous to mulch in autumn and top dress lightly in spring with bone meal, at least until well established.
PROPAGATION
By division in spring or autumn, or by

Colchicum autumnale 'Alba'

sowing fresh seed in a soil-based compost at about 20°C (68°F); germination is slow. Named varieties generally do not come true from seed.

PROBLEMS

Slugs and snails.

RECOMMENDED VARIETIES

The normal species is easily the most frequently seen form but others, generally less invasive and vigorous, are 'Albostriata' (which masquerades under other similar names, too) with golden-striped leaves, 'Fortin's Giant' with particularly tall stems and large leaves, and *rosea* with pink flowers (which never really look right).

Cyclamen

❝ Everyone knows cyclamen, although few realise that they belong to the primula family and are, therefore, dicotyledons and quite unrelated to lilies and other familiar bulbs. Most cyclamen bought today are the large-flowered, non-hardy hybrids growing in pots in people's houses, and I count this a great pity for their pink- or white-flowered hardy relatives from western Asia and southern Europe form the most exquisite leaf and flower carpet in some fairly inhospitable parts of my shade garden. I hope you will come to appreciate them too but, above all, with hardy cyclamen, do be sure that you buy stock that has been raised in cultivation – more than with almost any other plant, the wild populations of some cyclamen have been seriously depleted. ❞

Cyclamen hederifolium

PLANTING

As tubers (still sometimes called corms) during the dormant season, preferably towards autumn as root growth is beginning. I still find it more reliable to plant them first into small pots of humus-rich, soil-based compost and then move them into the garden after six months or so when growth is well underway. Plant with the top of the tuber just beneath the soil surface.

CARE

Once established, little care is necessary, but they will spread much more effectively if they are top dressed when dormant with leaf mould to which a little bone meal has been added.

PROPAGATION

By removal and replanting of daughter tubers or self-sown seedlings or by ripe

---

SHADE TOLERANCE Light to moderate, preferably dappled under deciduous trees.
SOIL Many, provided it is well-drained and preferably rich in leaf mould but tolerant of considerable dryness, especially when dormant.
HARDINESS Hardy, tolerating at least -20°C (-4°F).
SIZE Up to 10cm (4in).

(dark-coloured) seed sown shallowly in a soil-based, humus-rich seedling compost at about 15°C (60°F). Germination is fairly slow and erratic.

PROBLEMS

Vine weevil larvae can be very destructive of the tubers.

RECOMMENDED VARIETIES

There are two really important hardy cyclamen species, both equally prized for their flowers and foliage. The commonest and least expensive is the autumn-flowering *Cyclamen hederifolium* (formerly *C. neapolitanum*) which is variable in its foliage, and selected colour forms are sometimes offered. The white-flowered variety 'Alba' is lovely. The winter- and spring-flowering *C. coum* is always more costly and, similarly, occurs in a range of colour variants; and also has a white-flowered variety, 'Alba'. Among other reliably hardy species, I have been most successful with the spring-flowering *C. repandum*, the summer to autumn-flowering *C. purpurascens* (also called *C. europaeum*) which is the only fragrant hardy species, and the autumn-flowering *C. cilicium*.

BULBS

Eranthis Winter aconite

It is an unfortunate gardening confusion that the winter aconite is Eranthis hyemalis *and not* Aconitum *(a fairly closely-related genus), but it is, nonetheless, among the plants that I believe* should be in every garden. I find its bright yellow buttercup flowers sitting on a ruff of delicate ferny foliage are among the most welcome signs that spring is around the corner.*

PLANTING

Preferably in full leaf after flowering although it may only be possible to obtain dormant tubers which are difficult to establish in some soils. Position tubers about 4-5cm (1½-2in) deep. Grows well among grass.

CARE

Little needed, fading foliage may be pulled away but it is useful to top dress lightly in spring with bone meal.

PROPAGATION

Best by removal of the numerous self-sown seedlings or alternatively by the division of clumps immediately after flowering. Fresh seed should be sown very shallowly in a soil-based seedling compost and will then germinate quickly at a temperature of approximately 15-20°C (60-68°F).

PROBLEMS

None.

SHADE TOLERANCE Light to moderate.
SOIL Most, provided it is well-drained; tolerant of considerable dryness and drought tolerant when dormant.
HARDINESS Hardy, tolerating -20°C (-4°F).
SIZE Up to about 15cm (6in); more in good conditions.

RECOMMENDED VARIETIES
Usually only the commonest species is available, although sometimes selected sterile hybrid forms called Tubergenii or 'Guinea Gold' may be offered.

Eranthus hyemalis

Erythronium Dog's-tooth violets

Among all of the plants in my shade garden, I am most surprised by the unfamiliarity of visitors with these delightful spring-flowering bulbs, the nodding flowers of which have a 'swept-back' look. The leaves are lush and unexpectedly broad for a bulbous liliaceous plant – and delightfully spotted in the commonest species. I can think of no greater pleasure than chancing upon a clump of erythroniums in a cool, moist, shaded bed.

SHADE TOLERANCE Moderate.
SOIL Cool and moist but well-drained and humus-rich.
HARDINESS Moderately hardy to hardy, tolerating -15 to -20°C (5 to -4°F).
SIZE Flower stalk up to about 30cm (12in).

PLANTING

As bulbs (often called tubers), with the base at a depth of about 15cm (6in).

CARE

Little needed, but it is advantageous to mulch in autumn and top dress lightly in spring with bone meal.

PROPAGATION

By division of bulb clumps when dormant, or by sowing fresh seed in a humus-rich, soil-based compost at about 20°C (68°F); germination is fairly slow. Named varieties generally do not come true from seed.

PROBLEMS

Slugs.

Erythronium oregonum

RECOMMENDED VARIETIES
Erythronium dens-canis is the commonest of the types and arguably the loveliest of all. Another widely grown form is the very pale yellow-flowered hybrid 'Pagoda'.

Fritillaria

❝ There are two fairly distinctive groups of fritillary; all will arouse comment and, by and large, admiration. On the one hand there is the fairly low-growing native snake's head with its nodding bell-like flowers, and on the other, the taller forms, mostly from western Asia, of which the imposing crown imperials are the best known. Snake's heads generally fare best in the sun, but among the taller species are some useful plants for lightly shaded areas at the edge of a woodland garden. ❞

SHADE TOLERANCE Light.
SOIL Deep, rich, moisture retentive but not prone to waterlogging.
HARDINESS Very hardy, tolerating at least -20°C (-4°F).
SIZE Flower stalk grows up to 1.5m (5ft).

PLANTING

As bulbs, on their sides (to prevent water collecting in the hollow on top), about 15-20cm (6-8in) deep.

CARE

Mulch in autumn and early spring and top dress lightly in spring with bone meal. Do not disturb, once established, unless absolutely necessary.

Fritillaria imperialis

PROPAGATION

By division of bulb clumps in spring or autumn or by sowing fresh seed in a soil-based compost at about 20°C (68°F); germination is slow.

PROBLEMS

Slugs.

RECOMMENDED VARIETIES
Fritillaria imperialis is the crown imperial, of which there are several varieties, some with red-orange and some with yellow flowers. Among other easily obtained species, *F. persica*, with a spike of deep purple bell-like flowers, has thrived well for me beneath deciduous trees and others are worth experimenting with.

BULBS

Galanthus Snowdrop

6 6 *If snowdrops appeared in summer, they would have far fewer fans than they have now. Yes, I'm sure that it is their appearance in winter, convincing gardeners there is a spring somewhere in the future, that has elevated snowdrops into the highest echelons of everyone's affections. They are easy to grow but few gardeners appreciate how wide a range of variation exists, especially in overall height. Visitors to my garden just don't believe that the 45cm (18in) tall flowers by the front door are snowdrops at all.* 9 9

PLANTING

As growing plants, just after the flowers have faded – commonly called 'in the green'. Experience has proved that the plants establish and flower more quickly from this start than from dry bulbs in the autumn, and many nurseries now supply them in this way. In

RECOMMENDED VARIETIES

The common snowdrop is *Galanthus nivalis* and there is nothing at all wrong with it; it is certainly the least expensive form. Among others commonly seen are its double form, 'Flore Pleno', and a variant called 'Viridapicis', with markedly green outer flower parts. Among the tall forms, the best are *G.* x *atkinsii* (the one by my front door) and *G.* 'Sam Arnott'. Specialist nurseries stock many more, some very expensive and often with obscure special appeal.

SHADE TOLERANCE
Moderate to fairly deep.
SOIL Many, provided it is well-drained and preferably rich in leaf mould.
HARDINESS Very hardy, tolerating at least -20°C (-4°F).
SIZE Up to 45cm (18in), depending on variety.

any event, plant bulbs with their base about 10cm (4in) deep.

CARE

Little care needed but a top dressing with bone meal or general fertilizer while in full leaf is beneficial.

PROPAGATION

By division and replanting (see left) or as ripe seed sown shallowly in a soil-based seedling compost at 15-20°C (60-68°F). Germination is fairly slow and erratic.

PROBLEMS

None.

Hyacinthoides Bluebell

6 6 *For me, the bluebell has only one drawback: it is invasive and, in appropriate conditions and in small gardens, it can take on an almost weed-like quality. But for anyone with a shaded corner under trees where it can be allowed free rein, it really is an absolute must for its almost ethereal springtime colour. In the mass there seems to be nothing bluer.* 9 9

SHADE TOLERANCE
Moderate to deep.
SOIL Most; tolerant of wetter soils than most bulbs and will thrive even in fairly heavy clay.
HARDINESS Very hardy, tolerating below -20°C (-4°F).
SIZE About 50cm (20in).

Galanthus nivalis 'Flore Pleno'

Hyacinthoides non-scripta

PLANTING

As dormant bulbs in autumn, with their base ideally about 15cm (6in) deep, or as plants after division of clumps in spring. But the bluebell is really so easy to establish that even plants tossed onto the soil surface will generally root.

CARE

Little needed but the old leaves and flower stalks may be pulled away and the plants mulched and top dressed lightly with bone meal in early spring.

PROPAGATION

By division of bulb clumps, either immediately after flowering or when dormant, or by removal of the numerous self-sown seedlings. Fresh seed should be sown shallowly in soil-based seedling compost and will germinate fairly quickly at 15-20°C (60-68°F).

PROBLEMS

Rust.

RECOMMENDED VARIETIES
The common bluebell is *Hyacinthoides non-scripta* and most gardeners will be very happy with this, but there are white- and pink-flowered variants too.

Iris foetidissima
Stinking gladwyn

6 6 *This is the only really shade-tolerant species among the entire* Iris *genus, and what a special plant it is. Its main attractions are its tolerance of dry shade and its bright orange seeds that shine like jewels when the pods split open in the autumn but, unlike most gardeners, I also find appeal and interest in the small yellowish-purple flowers. Yes, a lovely and very useful plant; pity about the name.* 9 9

SHADE TOLERANCE
Moderate to deep.
SOIL Most, including dry.
HARDINESS Very hardy, tolerating at least -20°C (-4°F).
SIZE Flower stalk up to about 90cm (36in).

PLANTING
As plants, to the soil mark at the stem base or, as dormant rhizomes, at a depth of about 15cm (6in).

CARE
Little needed, but it is advantageous to mulch in autumn and top dress lightly in spring; I have found potassium sulphate gives excellent results and encourages good flower and seed production.

PROPAGATION
By sowing fresh seed in a humus-rich, soil-based compost in autumn and leaving outside to overwinter, or by division of clumps in spring or autumn.

PROBLEMS
None.

RECOMMENDED VARIETIES
Only the true species is usually available although variegated foliage forms exist, and a variety called *Iris foetidissima citrina* with large, rich yellow flowers is a particularly fine plant.

Iris foetidissima

BULBS

Leucojum Snowflake

❝ *The reason why snowflakes are not as popular as snowdrops is understandable, for by the time they come into flower in spring, there are many other, brighter and more assertive plants in bloom. But for stateliness and majesty, the finest of the leucojums are a match for anything and they continue the appeal of their hanging white bells well into the summer. My shade garden would certainly be much the poorer without them.* ❞

SHADE TOLERANCE
Moderate.
SOIL Deep, rich, moisture retentive but not prone to waterlogging.
HARDINESS Hardy, tolerating -15 to -20°C (5 to -4°F).
SIZE In most species about 20cm (8in) but up to 75cm (30in) in *L. aestivum* 'Gravetye Giant'.

PLANTING
As bulbs with their base at a depth of about 15cm (6in).

CARE
Mulch in the autumn and early spring and then top dress lightly with bone meal in spring.

RECOMMENDED VARIETIES
Three fairly common species from central or southern Europe are *Leucojum vernum*, the so-called spring snowflake, which flowers in winter; *L. aestivum*, the summer snowflake, which flowers in spring and includes the tall variety 'Gravetye Giant'; and *L. autumnale*, flowering in late summer or autumn.

PROPAGATION
By division of bulb clumps in spring or autumn, or by sowing fresh seed in a soil-based compost at about 20°C (68°F); germination is slow.

PROBLEMS
None.

Leucojum aestivum 'Gravetye Giant'

Lilium Lily

❝ *There are a small number of plants that have truly majestic status. Lilies are their representatives among the bulbs and I have always believed that they should find a place in every garden, either in the open ground or, better to my mind, in pots. A number of different lilies will be happy at the very edge of the shade garden, and a few, slightly further in. It is, however, worth experimenting, especially with the species; they will always indicate if they are not at home in a shady situation as they will seek the light and their stems will bend accordingly. Grow them in pots and move them until the best position is found.* ❞

Lilium regale 'Album'

SHADE TOLERANCE Light, preferably dappled under deciduous trees.
SOIL Moist, fairly free-draining, rich, organic.
HARDINESS Moderately hardy to hardy, tolerating -10 to -20°C (14 to -4°F), if mulched.
SIZE Variable with species, about 75cm-2.5m (30in-8ft).

PLANTING

As dormant bulbs, as soon as possible after lifting. Ideally, this should be in the autumn, but it will usually be early spring before many are available in shops and nurseries. Plant promptly at a depth equal to at least three times the bulbs' diameter, which may mean 20cm (8in) or more deep, whether in pots or open ground. The one exception to deep planting is *Lilium martagon*, which should have its bulbs just below the surface of the soil.

CARE

Cut down dead stems as they fade in the autumn and mulch in spring, just

RECOMMENDED VARIETIES

The lilies that have succeeded best in the shade for me are species including the fabulous white and mauve *Lilium regale*; the yellow *L. hansonii*; the tall, orange *L. henryi*; the golden *L. auratum*; the variously orange-coloured varieties of *L. bulbiferum*; the white European Madonna lily, *L. martagon*; the yellow *L. monadelphum*; and the rich red tiger lily, *L. tigrinum*, but do try whatever others you have.

before new shoots appear, with leaf mould to which a scattering of bone meal has been added. Leave undisturbed for as long as possible.

PROPAGATION

By division of clumps and replanting of daughter bulbs, as seed (of true species only, not hybrids) sown shallowly in a soil-based seedling compost at 15-20°C (60-68°F) (germination with many species is generally fairly swift), in a few cases as bulbils, planted in the same way as seed, or as bulb scales, pulled away and potted up in a warm propagator.

PROBLEMS

Lily beetle, aphids, which must be controlled as they will otherwise bring virus (although this is generally not as severe on species as it is on hybrids), grey mould.

BULBS

Ornithogalum Star of Bethlehem

❝ This is an easy-to-grow yet, with one exception, a surprisingly unfamiliar genus of predominantly white-flowered bulbs, mostly from the Mediterranean and eastern Asia. The exception is the one to avoid: Ornithogalum umbellatum *is an invasive plant that is much too easy, and can quickly become an almost ineradicable weed. Choose its better-disciplined, rather more stately relatives with taller spikes that bear masses of tiny white star-like flowers in late spring.* ❞

SHADE TOLERANCE Light, preferably dappled.
SOIL Most, but best in well-drained, fairly organic soils.
HARDINESS Fairly hardy to very hardy (depending on species), tolerating -5 to -20°C (23 to -4°F).
SIZE Flower spike 30-50cm (12-20in), depending on species.

PLANTING
As dormant bulbs in autumn, with their base 7-8cm (2½-3in) deep and at least 20cm (8in) apart.
CARE
Mulch in early spring with fine compost and top dress lightly with bone meal.
PROPAGATION
By division of bulb clumps when dormant, or by removal of offsets when in growth, or as seed. Sow fresh seed very shallowly in soil-based seedling compost outdoors or in a cold frame. Germination is usually slow – nine months or more may elapse before they emerge from dormancy.
PROBLEMS
None.

RECOMMENDED VARIETIES
The loveliest species for shade is *Ornithogalum narbonense*, up to 50cm (20in), although it isn't the hardiest, and in colder areas you will succeed better with *O. montanum* and *O. nutans*, both 30cm (12in). They naturalize readily and easily but I find they never become out of hand.

Scilla Squill

❝ *Long before I grew scillas in my own garden, I remember seeing a carpet of the short, astonishingly electric-blue spikes of* Scilla verna *on an exposed Welsh cliff-top. The image stayed with me and I was subsequently amazed to discover that plants that so revelled in the bright open sunshine would be equally happy in the partial shade beneath some of my lower-growing shrubs. But happy they are, and each spring I look forward to these easy and reliable signs of a new season.* ❞

SHADE TOLERANCE Light, dappled.
SOIL Most, tolerant of fairly dry soils but not of waterlogging, although always best in a free-draining, fairly rich loam.
HARDINESS Hardy, tolerating -20°C (-4°F).
SIZE Flower stalk up to about 15cm (6in).

PLANTING
As dormant bulbs, with their base about 4cm (1½ in) deep.
CARE
Little needed; they are almost too small to mulch but a light dressing with either bone meal or a general fertilizer in spring is advantageous.
PROPAGATION
By division of clumps in spring or autumn, or by removing some of the many self-sown seedlings. Seed may also be sown fresh in a soil-based compost in late spring and left outside.
PROBLEMS
None.

Ornithogalum montanum

RECOMMENDED VARIETIES

The loveliest and easiest species is the commonest – *Scilla siberica* – and this is the plant that has succeeded well for me in light shade. The best form is 'Spring Beauty', which looks lovely with the white 'Alba', but it would be worth experimenting with the others too.

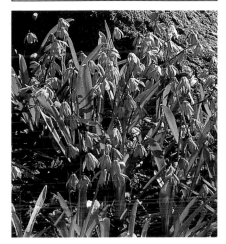

Scilla siberica 'Atrocoerulea'

Trillium Wood Lily

❝ *I read recently a gardener's complaint that if these plants weren't called wood lilies they would be more popular. I fail to see why, for they are truly members of the lily family and they truly live in woods although, admittedly, the name* Trillium *does convey more accurately their conspicuous appearance, with their parts in most attractive groups of three. But, yet again, they are not well known and mine never let me down, eliciting comment and admiration every spring.* ❞

Trillium grandiflorum

SHADE TOLERANCE
Moderate to deep, but preferably dappled.
SOIL Deep, humus-rich, moisture retentive.
HARDINESS Moderately hardy, tolerating -10 to -15°C (14-5°F).
SIZE In most species, about 30cm (12in).

PLANTING
As dormant rhizomes in autumn with their base at a depth of about 15-20cm (6-8in), or from pots as plants in growth.
CARE
Mulch in autumn and early spring. Top dress lightly with bone meal in spring.
PROPAGATION
By division of rhizomes in autumn or after flowering in spring, or by sowing

RECOMMENDED VARIETIES

The commonest species is the white-flowered North American *Trillium grandiflorum*, which occurs in a splendid double form, *flore-pleno*. But there are also many other species available from specialist suppliers. Look out for the green-yellow-flowered *T. luteum*; the extraordinary deep purple *T. cuneatum*; the dark green and purple *T. undulatum*; and the green-flowered *T. recurvatum*. All have a rich, exotic appeal.

fresh seed in a humus-rich, soil-based compost outdoors or in a cold frame. Germination should occur within about six months.
PROBLEMS
None.

ALPINES

Campanula Bellflower

❝ *The bellflowers will be known to every gardener, and the genus* Campanula *contains plants for many different situations. Among the rock garden species are some aggressive individuals, such as* Campanula portenschlagiana, *although these tend to be sun loving. But among the group are one or two European species that have performed well for me at the shadier end of my own rock garden; the little mat-forming* C. cochleariifolia *is one and the unexpectedly yellow-flowered and taller* C. thyrsoides *is another.* ❞

PLANTING
As plants from pots from spring to autumn.

SHADE TOLERANCE Light.
SOIL Slightly organic, well-drained.
HARDINESS Very hardy, tolerating at least -20°C (-4°F).
SIZE Variable with species, but about 15-40cm (6-16in).

CARE
Little needed but they will benefit from a light top dressing with bone meal or general fertilizer in early spring.

PROPAGATION
By careful division in spring or early summer, or by seed. *C. thyrsoides* is monocarpic – after two or three years as a rosette it flowers and then dies – so it is important to save seed as it won't reliably self-sow in all soils. Sow ripe seed in soil-based compost in autumn in a cold frame, and germination will usually take place in spring.

PROBLEMS
None.

RECOMMENDED VARIETIES
There are no selected varieties of *Campanula thyrsoides*, but a number of selections exist of *C. cochleariifolia*, among which the double 'Flore Pleno' and the finely coloured 'Oakington Blue' are particularly worth growing. Other alpine species reputedly tolerant of light shade include the more or less creeping *C. petrophila* and the rather taller *C. tommasiniana*, but I have no personal experience of this.

Chiastophyllum

❝ *The relative scarcity of shade-tolerant alpines means that among those that can be recommended are some from genera familiar only to the dedicated alpine gardener.* Chiastophyllum *from the Caucasus, in the family Crassulaceae, is one of them. But this little yellow-flowered, rosette-forming succulent is one of the most dependable plants for shady corners among rocks. The flowers are relatively unusual among alpines in comprising masses of tiny star-like blooms clustered on pendulous catkin-like inflorescences.* ❞

SHADE TOLERANCE Light, ideally in rock crevices.
SOIL Free-draining, slightly gritty but with some organic matter.
HARDINESS Hardy to very hardy, tolerating -20°C (-4°F).
SIZE Flower stalk to 15cm (6in).

Campanula portenschlagiana

Chiastophyllum oppositifolium

PLANTING

As plants from pots from spring to autumn.

CARE

Trim off dead flower stalks after flowering. Lightly top dress with bone meal in early spring.

PROPAGATION

By division in spring or summer or by side-shoot cuttings in spring. Seed may be sown outdoors in gritty soil-based compost in autumn, and will usually germinate in spring.

PROBLEMS

None.

RECOMMENDED VARIETIES

There is only one species, *Chiastophyllum oppositifolium*, although a selected form called 'Jim's Pride' is claimed to be better (at least by Jim).

Gentiana Gentian

❝ *There can be no more admired rock garden plant than the gentian, although as a group gentians have the reputation of being tricky to grow and even trickier to flower. This is true of some of the species but not, in my experience, of those that are likely to interest the shade gardener. The almost magical blue of the trumpet-shaped gentian flower is legendary, although there are white-, purple-, red- and even yellow-flowered species too. In case you become lost among the mass of species, a good rule of thumb is that most of the North American, Himalayan and other eastern Asian types are shade tolerant, most of the European and New Zealand species less so. But there are exceptions.* ❞

SHADE TOLERANCE Light, dappled.
SOIL Fairly organic, slightly acid, moisture retentive but not waterlogged.
HARDINESS Hardy to very hardy, tolerating -20°C (-4°F).
SIZE Variable with species, from more or less stemless to 60cm (24in).

PLANTING

As plants from pots from spring to autumn.

CARE

Little needed, but the taller species benefit from having the dead flower stalks trimmed off after flowering. Lightly top dress with bone meal in early spring.

RECOMMENDED VARIETIES

Among about 400 species, I must restrict myself only to those of which I have experience, but suggest that in choosing others you follow my rule of thumb (outlined left). The following have performed well in shade for me: *Gentiana makinoi* blue flowers at the tips of 60cm (24in) long stalks; *G. sino-ornata* single blue flowers on creeping stems; *G. asclepiadea* willow gentian, blue flowers in leaf axils on arching, 60cm (24in) long stems; and *G. andrewsii* blue flowers in clusters at the ends of 30cm (12in) stems.

Gentiana sino-ornata

PROPAGATION

By division in spring or early summer, by semi-ripe cuttings in summer, or by seed. Sow ripe seed in slightly humus-rich, soil-based compost in autumn in a cold frame, and germination will usually take place in spring.

PROBLEMS

None.

ALPINES

Oxalis

❝ Perhaps it's because an Oxalis *was the first rock garden plant that I ever bought that it has such a special place in my affections. But this is a real Jekyll and Hyde genus that includes* Oxalis corniculata, *arguably the most ineradicable garden weed, as well as my plant, the compact and very well-disciplined South American* O. adenophylla, *with its glaucous leaves and pretty pink flowers. Although not strictly a rock plant, I also include here the European wood sorrel,* O. acetosella. ❞*

PLANTING
As plants from pots from spring to autumn.

CARE
Little needed, but they will benefit from a light top dressing with bone meal or general fertilizer in early spring.

SHADE TOLERANCE Light to moderate, preferably dappled.
SOIL Best in fairly organic, slightly acid and moisture retentive.
HARDINESS Very hardy, tolerating at least -20°C (-4°F).
SIZE Variable with species, but up to about 15cm (6in).

PROPAGATION
By division or offsets in spring or early summer, or by seed. Sow ripe seed in slightly humus-rich, soil-based compost in autumn in a cold frame, and germination will usually take place in spring.

PROBLEMS
None.

RECOMMENDED VARIETIES
Several species in addition to *Oxalis adenophylla* and *O. acetosella* are sometimes offered and are suitable for shade. Among those most likely to be seen are the North American wood sorrels, *O. oregana* and *O. violacea*.

Oxalis adenophylla

Phlox

❝ Phlox *is another big genus that embraces the herbaceous border and the annual bed as well as the rock garden. Most of the dwarf alpine* Phlox *are sun loving, but there is one notable exception in the delicious little pink-flowered form of* Phlox adsurgens. *It has very pretty saucer-shaped flowers with overlapping petals. It is a creeping species, but in my experience never invasively so, and is a very useful plant for those difficult spots that occur in any reasonably sized alpine garden.* ❞

SHADE TOLERANCE Light.
SOIL Preferably slightly organic, moist but free-draining.
HARDINESS Very hardy, tolerating at least -20°C (-4°F).
SIZE Some shoots will reach 30cm (12in) but most flop below this height.

PLANTING
As plants from pots from spring to autumn.

CARE
Little needed, but it is advantageous to lightly trim back wayward shoots after flowering in late summer and apply a light top dressing with bone meal or general fertilizer in spring.

PROPAGATION
By layering or removal of already rooted stems in spring, or by seed. Sow ripe seed in slightly humus-rich, soil-based compost in autumn in a cold frame; germination is fairly slow.

PROBLEMS
None.

Phlox adsurgens 'Wagon Wheel'

RECOMMENDED VARIETIES

There are some selected forms of *Phlox adsurgens* of which the best are 'Wagon Wheel' pink flowers, rounded leaves, 'Red Buttes' large, deep pink flowers, and 'Black Buttes' mauve flowers.

ALPINES

Primula

❝ *There can be few more loved garden (or wild) plants than primroses, and the huge genus, Primula, to which they belong contains a number of indispensable species for the shaded rock garden. Because the group is so large and rather diverse, however, I've also included here for convenience a few primulas that are more accurately described as dwarf herbaceous perennials; but whatever you prefer to call them, grow some, and your shaded beds will be much the lovelier.* ❞

PLANTING
As plants from pots from spring to autumn.

CARE
Little needed but it is beneficial to apply a light top dressing with bone meal or general fertilizer in spring. Most primulas benefit from being divided every two or three years and the best time to do this is immediately after flowering.

SHADE TOLERANCE Light to moderate.

SOIL Varies with species but most rock garden types will thrive in very slightly organic but predominantly gritty, moist though free-draining soil. Types for other beds are generally best in very slightly acid, humus-rich, moist but not waterlogged soil. As conditions vary and some of the most choice species have particular requirements, do check when buying from specialist suppliers.

HARDINESS Very hardy, tolerating at least -20°C (-4°F).

SIZE Varies with species, with flowers stalks ranging from 2-3cm (1in) to almost 1m (3ft).

RECOMMENDED VARIETIES
To be honest, most types of *Primula* will survive at least in light shade, but some are far better in shade and a few almost require it. In short, therefore, almost any are worthy of experimentation but the following is a list drawn from my own experience:

For the shaded rock garden: *Primula parryi, P. ellisiae* and *P. involucrata.*

For other shaded beds: Primrose types, such as *P. vulgaris* (primrose), *P. elatior* (oxslip), *P. vulgaris and P. juliae* hybrids (such as 'Wanda'), and hybrids of polyanthus type; *Candelabra primulas;* Himalayan cowslip types, such as *P. sikkimensis; P. vialii; P. rosea;* and drumstick primulas of *P. denticulata* type.

Among those that, in my experience, are not really worth attempting to grow as they require more sun are auriculas and the bird's-eye primulas, such as *P. farinosa, P. marginata* and *P. veris* (cowslip).

PROPAGATION
By division, or by sowing ripe seed on the surface of a slightly organic soil-based compost. After sowing, the seed should be kept somewhere cool because germination is suppressed at temperatures above approximately 20°C (68°F). Germination tends to be slow as well as erratic, and the seedlings should be pricked out as they emerge, which may be over a period of several months.

PROBLEMS
Slugs.

Primula vulgaris

Saxifraga

" If one plant can be said to sum up rock gardening, it must be the saxifrage; although to talk of a genus of approaching 400 species as 'one plant' is a trifle misleading. There are several well-defined groups varying in habit from close, rock-hugging mats to much more upright clumps. A few can be used as genuine border plants, but most are more at home in the rock garden or a special moist shade bed where their massed, but individually tiny flowers in a wide range of colours will always attract attention. "

SHADE TOLERANCE Light to moderate.
SOIL Varies with species, but most rock garden types will thrive in slightly organic but predominantly gritty, moist though free-draining soil. As with primulas, however, conditions vary and some of the most choice species have particular requirements, so do check when buying from specialist suppliers.
HARDINESS Very hardy, tolerating at least -20°C (-4°F).
SIZE Varies with species, with flowers stalks ranging from 2-3cm (1in) to 20-30cm (8-12in).

PLANTING

As plants from pots from spring to autumn.

CARE

Little needed, but it is advantageous to apply a light top dressing with bone meal or general fertilizer in spring.

Saxifraga **'Cloth of Gold'**

PROPAGATION

Most reliably by division, or by small softwood cuttings taken immediately after flowering. The seeds are very tiny and should be sown when ripe on the surface of a gritty soil-based compost. Germination, with most species, is slow and erratic and will generally only take place after the seed pans have been left with minimal protection over winter in a cold frame. Bringing them into slight artificial warmth of around 10°C (50°F) in spring may be beneficial in speeding up germination. As an alternative to the overwintering, the seed pans may be placed in a fridge for about two months.

PROBLEMS

None.

RECOMMENDED VARIETIES

As with primulas, most types of saxifrage will tolerate some shade and many require it. The principle group that will not be successful is that of the close, mat-forming encrusted types which must have full sun. Among the many others that have given special pleasure in the shadier parts of my rock garden are the large group of mossy saxifrages, but these represent only one part of this large and wonderful genus.

CLIMBERS

Akebia quinata Chocolate Vine

It's because really interesting shade-tolerant climbers are so few and far between that I have included Akebia, *although its greatest appeal lies with the curious deep purple and spicy scented flowers that are reliably produced only in warm seasons. Even more occasionally, greyish sausage-like fruits will be produced, too, but lest I am putting you off with my cautionary words, be assured that the five-lobed leaves, that are certainly produced every year, will add interest and grace to any woodland garden.*

SHADE TOLERANCE Light to moderate, preferably dappled.
SOIL Preferably a humus-rich, moisture-retentive loam.
HARDINESS Fairly hardy, tolerating -10°C (14°F).
SIZE 2m (6ft) after three years, up to 12m (40ft) eventually.

CARE
Give some protection in the first winter after planting, mulch in autumn and spring, preferably with leaf mould, and give a balanced general fertilizer in spring. *Akebia* is a twiner that can be supported on any fairly informal structure, such as an old tree or strong wires on a wall.

PROPAGATION
By semi-ripe cuttings in late summer in a sand and peat mixture, or by layering.

PRUNING
Not normally necessary, but old and overgrown plants will regenerate after being cut back hard in spring.

PROBLEMS
None.

RECOMMENDED VARIETIES
Only the true species is available.

Clematis

It's impossible to write or talk of climbing plants for the garden without the name Clematis *coming up fairly quickly. This charming genus includes some quite beautifully flowered plants for almost every garden situation, although shade tolerance is perhaps the attribute least commonly associated with them. I've considered* Clematis *at some length in* Best Climbers, *Book 1 of this series and so I shall restrict myself here to the two groups that I have found most successful in shade: the early-flowered species,* Clematis alpina, *and the late-flowered species,* C. viticella *and* C. tangutica, *although it's worth adding that many of the very popular summer-flowering hybrids offer their best flower-colour when the head of the plant is lightly shaded.*

SHADE TOLERANCE Light to moderate, preferably dappled.
SOIL Preferably a humus-rich, moist, slightly alkaline loam.
HARDINESS Hardy to very hardy, tolerating -20°C (-4°F).
SIZE *C. alpina* 2-3m (6-10ft)), late-flowering species 4-5m (13-16ft) .

Clematis 'Madame Julia Correvon'

CARE
Plant deeply, at least 15cm (6in) below the soil level indicated on the stem, to lessen the likelihood of clematis wilt. Mulch in autumn and spring with well-rotted manure or garden compost and give a top dressing with a balanced general fertilizer in early spring. *Clematis* are tendril climbers and may be given formal or informal support. Of those that are included here, the early-flowering species are perhaps best on a trellis attached to a wall, while the later-flowering species are best growing through trees or large shrubs.

PROPAGATION

Easiest by semi-ripe cuttings taken inter-nodally in late summer.

PRUNING

Varies considerably between sub-groups within the genus. Of those described here, the early-flowering species should be lightly pruned either before or after blooming in spring; the later-flowering species should be pruned hard in early spring to a pair of buds about 75cm (30in) above soil level.

PROBLEMS

Slugs, mildew and clematis wilt.

RECOMMENDED VARIETIES

Clematis alpina 'Frances Rivis' large, pale blue, 'Rosy Pagoda' pale pink, 'White Moth' double white; *C. viticella* 'Mme Julia Correvon' dark red, 'Royal Velours' deep purple, 'Purpurea Plena Elegans' double, violet-purple; *C. tangutica* and related types 'Gravetye Variety' yellow, 'Orange Peel' orange, markedly thickened sepals, 'Bill Mackenzie' yellow.

Hedera Ivy

❝ *There is no plant, climber or not, whose very name is more redolent of shady places than the ivy. As cover for unsightly structures, as decorative feature plants over purpose-made supports or as invaluable evergreen carpeting ground cover, they have no rivals. And perish the oft-made comment that they are dull, for among the innumerable varieties are some of the prettiest and daintiest variegated foliage plants you will see anywhere.* ❞

SHADE TOLERANCE

Moderate to deep (especially green, small-leaved forms).

SOIL Most, including dry but always best in rich loam.

HARDINESS Hardy to very hardy, many tolerating at least -20°C (-4°F).

SIZE Very variable, depending on variety, so check when buying; some will reach at least 15m (50ft) in 10 years.

CARE

Established plants need little attention, but in the early stages they will benefit from mulching at least once a year and feeding in spring with a balanced general fertilizer. Ivies have clinging aerial roots and require no tying-in.

PROPAGATION

Easiest by layering but an alternative is to propagate by using semi-ripe cuttings in late summer.

PRUNING

None needed, although they are usually neatest when lightly trimmed in spring.

RECOMMENDED VARIETIES

There are two main groups of ivies: the small-leaved types, of which the native *Hedera helix* is much the most important, and the large-leaved, generally slightly less hardy ones, *H. colchica* and *H. canariensis*. Among the former, I am especially fond of 'Goldheart' green leaves with golden central blotch, 'Parsley Crested' green leaves with wavy margin, 'Glacier' green and silvery leaves, less vigorous, and 'Buttercup' golden yellow, especially when young. Among larger-leaved types, there are none better than 'Sulphur Heart' pale green leaves with paler green and yellow blotches, and 'Gloire de Marengo' dark green leaves with silver-grey surround and white margins, vigorous.

They will regenerate after hard cutting back but do so rather slowly.

PROBLEMS

None.

Hedera helix 'Goldheart'

CLIMBERS

Hydrangea petiolaris Climbing hydrangea

" This isn't the only climbing hydrangea but it is certainly the best known, easiest to obtain and probably the hardiest. It is also a very useful and vigorous plant, albeit deciduous, for covering a large shaded wall. It could equally be grown up a large tree, but it is as a wall plant that it has its greatest merit. The appeal lies in the self-clinging habit, copper-coloured winter bark, the fresh green leaves and the modest but, nonetheless, pretty summer flowers. "

CARE

I find it an advantage to peg young shoots to the wall to ensure that the surface is ultimately covered uniformly. Mulch in autumn and spring and give a balanced general fertilizer in spring.

SHADE TOLERANCE Light to moderate or almost deep.
SOIL A rich, moisture-retentive deep loam is needed for real success.
HARDINESS Hardy, tolerating -15°C (5°F).
SIZE 3m (10ft) after three years, up to 20m (60ft) eventually.

RECOMMENDED VARIETIES
Normal species only available.

PROPAGATION
Semi-hardwood cuttings in late summer.
PRUNING
None needed, but if outgrowing its allotted space, it may be cut back as hard as necessary in spring.
PROBLEMS
None.

Hydrangea petiolaris

Lapageria rosea Chilean bell flower

" The Chilean bell flower isn't a common plant or a particularly hardy one, for it has specific soil requirements. But it is such a gem when grown well that I do feel it should be in every shade garden that offers the appropriate conditions. It has crimson, bell-like flowers in late summer that are elegantly set off against dark evergreen foliage. It is the national flower of Chile, and once seen you will soon appreciate the wisdom of this choice. "

CARE

Must be grown in a fairly warm, shel-

SHADE TOLERANCE Light to moderate, preferably dappled.
SOIL Best in rich, organic, acid loam.
HARDINESS Barely hardy, tolerating -5°C (23°F).
SIZE 1m (3ft) after three years, up to 5m (16ft) eventually.

tered position and even then requires protection during the first winter after planting. Mulch in autumn and spring, preferably with an acidic leaf mould. Give a balanced general or rose fertilizer in spring. The Chilean bell flower is a twiner that should be supported on horizontal wires.

PROPAGATION
Easiest by layering in late autumn or winter. May be raised from seed provided it is fresh and washed free of its jelly-like coat. Sow in a soil-based compost at around 20°C (68°F). Germinates within about three months.
PRUNING
Not normally necessary, but may be lightly pruned to shape in spring.
PROBLEMS
Aphids.

RECOMMENDED VARIETIES
'Albiflora' white, 'Beatrice Anderson' deep red, 'Nash Court' deep pink.

Lonicera Honeysuckle

❝ *Probably the best known and best loved of all climbers and certainly one of the best for shade, but only really successful in a relatively wild situation. The scrambling habit just isn't neat and tidy enough for trellis on the house wall of a meticulous small modern garden, and the vigour of most types will envelop small sheds and other outbuildings.* ❞

SHADE TOLERANCE Light to moderate.
SOIL Best in deep rich, organic loam; never successful in very dry sites.
HARDINESS Most are hardy, tolerating at least -15°C (5°F).
SIZE Varies between species, from about 3m (10ft) eventually (L. x heckrottii) to 5m (16ft) or more.

CARE
Mulch in autumn and spring and give balanced rose or other potassium-rich fertilizer in spring.

PROPAGATION
Layer in autumn or take semi-ripe cuttings of the current year's shoots in a soil-based compost in late summer. Most of the best varieties don't come true from seed.

PRUNING
Periodically, in spring, cut out the oldest and thickest shoots to encourage new growth.

PROBLEMS
Aphids, mildew.

RECOMMENDED VARIETIES
The full range of garden honeysuckles is described in Book 1 of the series but my choices among the most important are *Lonicera periclymenum* 'Belgica' early summer, purple and red-yellow, fragrant; *L. caprifolium* summer, yellowish, fragrant, vigorous; *L. japonica* 'Halliana' summer, evergreen, yellow, fragrant; *L.* x *brownii* 'Dropmore Scarlet' rich red flowers until well into autumn, not fragrant; *L.* x *heckrottii* early, yellow, some fragrance, low vigour.

Parthenocissus

❝ *There is no more effective and neat cover for a shaded wall than a parthenocissus vine, be it the large-leaved and vigorous* Parthenocissus henryana *or the smaller-leaved and tightly adhering Boston ivy,* P. triscupidata, *that turns so fiery red in autumn before its leaves fall. And therein lies the drawback: they are deciduous and until established with a thick network of stems offer little interest in winter.* ❞

SHADE TOLERANCE Light to moderate.
SOIL Most, but better in fairly rich, moisture-retentive loam.
HARDINESS Most are hardy, tolerating at least -15°C (5°F).
SIZE Varies between species, from about 2m (6ft) after three years to 9m (30ft) eventually with *P. tricuspidata* and rather more with *P. henryana*.

Parthenocissus henryana

CARE
Mulch in autumn and spring with compost or leaf mould and give balanced general fertilizer in spring. They may take time before they climb and are best left to form a mound of growth at the base of the wall, from which vertical shoots will eventually arise.

PROPAGATION
Layer in autumn or take semi-ripe cuttings of the current year's shoots in a soil-based compost in late summer.

PRUNING
None essential, but shoots may be cut back as hard as necessary in spring to limit spread, as required.

PROBLEMS
None.

RECOMMENDED VARIETIES
Parthenocissus henryana large bronze-green leaves; *P. tricuspidata* 'Veitchii' the best form of the species with small, three-lobed reddish-purple leaves; *P. quinquefolia* five-lobed leaves, rather more open habit.

SHRUBS

Aucuba japonica
Spotted laurel

❝ *If there is one plant that I could not have left out of this book, Aucuba japonica is it. I have two plants, of different varieties, and they grow for me in the most shaded, difficult spots in my garden, beneath the shade of a fairly large beech tree. The soil is dry, and from late spring onwards it is extremely dark, but the rich evergreen leaves with their cream-coloured spots shine through it all; and one of the plants has rich red berries from autumn to spring.* ❞

CARE
Little needed, although ideally mulch at least once a year and give a balanced general or rose fertilizer in spring.

PROPAGATION
Easiest by softwood cuttings in early

SHADE TOLERANCE
Moderate to deep.
SOIL Almost any, acid, alkaline, dry or fairly wet.
HARDINESS Hardy, tolerating at least -20°C (-4°F).
SIZE 1 x 1m (3 x 3ft) after three years, up to 4 x 3.5m (13 x 11ft) eventually.

summer or by hardwood cuttings in winter, in a cold frame.

PRUNING
Not necessary, but may be cut back fairly hard in spring to reduce size.

PROBLEMS
None, although shoot tips sometimes blacken for no apparent reason.

RECOMMENDED VARIETIES
Aucuba japonica 'Crotonifolia' female, so develops berries, large more yellowish leaf blotches, 'Variegata' female, abundantly spotted.

Berberis
Barberry

❝ *As a genus,* Berberis *is one of the glories of the shrub garden, its evergreen species being particularly lovely. But it is a huge group, with many deciduous types, too, all characterized by masses of orange, yellow or dark red flowers, mainly in spring. While many of the deciduous types are best in full sun, there are a few, together with several evergreen species, that thrive well in a lightly shaded bed.* ❞

SHADE TOLERANCE Light to moderate, preferably dappled.
SOIL Almost any, although not very heavy and wet or very dry.
HARDINESS Hardy to very hardy, tolerating at least -15 to -25°C (5 to -13°F).
SIZE Varies with species (see right) from 50 x 50cm (20 x 20in) to 4 x 4m (13 x 13ft).

CARE
Mulch in autumn and spring, preferably with leaf mould. Give a balanced rose fertilizer in spring.

PROPAGATION
Easiest by semi-ripe cuttings in early autumn, hardwood cuttings in winter or, with many species, by layering.

PRUNING
Not necessary when grown as a free-standing shrub, although wayward shoots may be cut back in spring. If grown as a hedge, clip lightly in early autumn.

PROBLEMS
None.

Aucuba japonica '**Picturata**'

Berberis darwinii

RECOMMENDED VARIETIES (EVERGREEN UNLESS STATED)

Berberis darwinii the loveliest of all, vivid orange, neat small leaves, to 3 x 3m (10 x 10ft); *B. x carminea* deciduous, yellow, early summer, best is 'Pirate King' with dark red berries, to 4 x 4m (13 x 13ft); *B. julianae* pale yellow, elongated leaves, to 4 x 4m (13 x 13ft); *B. buxifolia* 'Nana' semi-evergreen, yellow, to 50 x 50cm (20 x 20in); *B. candidula* yellow, to 1 x 1m (3 x 3ft); *B. linearifolia* 'Orange King' rich orange, to 3 x 3m (10 x 10ft); *B. stenophylla* 'Claret Cascade' red-orange, to 3 x 3m (10 x 10ft), 'Corallina Compacta' coral pink, to 40 x 40cm (16 x 16in); *B. thunbergii* deciduous, many forms with red, pink or white flowers and many with reddish foliage and good autumn colours, vary from 50 x 50cm (20 x 20in) to 3 x 3m (10 x 10ft); *B. wilsoniae* deciduous, pale yellow, to 1.5 x 2.5 m (5 x 8ft).

Buxus sempervirens Box

❛❛ *The box is one of those remarkable plants that, from a simple description, sounds the dullest piece of vegetation ever created: small, rounded, dark, evergreen leaves, insignificant flowers, a pretty slow growth rate and a dense habit. Yet with care, with clipping and correct placing, it can assume a quiet majesty. And its shade tolerance means that it is undeniably very useful.* ❜❜

SHADE TOLERANCE
Moderate to deep.

SOIL Almost any, provided it is not very heavy and wet, highly lime tolerant.

HARDINESS Very hardy, tolerating -25°C (-13°F).

SIZE Slowly reaches about 5-6 x 5-6m (16-20 x 16-20ft), but will usually be clipped to much less.

CARE
Little is necessary, but it is best when mulched in autumn and spring. Give a balanced general fertilizer in spring.

PROPAGATION
By hardwood cuttings in late autumn.

PRUNING
Not necessary, but it always looks best when clipped, ideally once in mid-summer and again in early autumn. Box may be cut back fairly hard in spring but, unlike yew (with which it shares many features), doesn't regenerate well from very old wood.

PROBLEMS
Whiteflies, aphids, box sucker.

RECOMMENDED VARIETIES
The normal species has much to commend it for ordinary use, but for dwarf edging (not usually needed in shade), choose 'Suffruticosa'. Among numerous variegated forms, 'Elegantissima' is best, but none of these forms develop their best colour in the shade.

Buxus sempervirens

SHRUBS

Camellia

66 *There are those who would claim that the camellia is the queen of any shrubbery, shaded or not. And I'd find it hard to argue. But these exquisite oriental evergreens with their red, pink, white or cream flowers are among those plants that aren't merely shade tolerant; they must have both shade and also shelter from cold winds if they are to succeed.* 99

SHADE TOLERANCE Light to fairly deep.
SOIL Acidic, organic, free-draining but not prone to drying out.
HARDINESS Fairly to moderately hardy, tolerating -10°C (14°C).
SIZE Up to 1 x 1m (3 x 3ft) after three years, about 3-4 x 2-3m (10-13 x 6-10ft) eventually.

CARE
Mulch in autumn and spring, ideally with acidic, conifer-needle leaf mould. Give a balanced rose fertilizer and sequestrene in spring.

PROPAGATION
By leaf-bud cuttings in spring, or by semi-ripe cuttings in autumn.

PRUNING
None, but branches may be cut back and straggly shoots shortened after flowering in spring to maintain shape.

PROBLEMS
None.

RECOMMENDED VARIETIES

Camellia japonica 'Adolphe Audusson' deep red, semi-double, 'Elegans' peach pink, anemone-flowered, 'Cornish Snow' white, single, small, 'Leonard Messel' peach pink, loosely paeony-flowered; *C. x williamsii* 'Donation' deep pink, semi-double.

Cornus canadensis Creeping dogwood

66 *Although some of the full-sized dogwoods can be grown in light shade, I never feel they seem very happy in these conditions, quite unlike their unexpectedly soil-hugging relative, which is one of the finest ground-cover plants for any woodland garden. It is always best in slightly milder areas where it will remain evergreen, but in any locality the delightful flowers with their four striking white bracts will form an entrancing carpet.* 99

SHADE TOLERANCE Light to moderate.
SOIL Tolerates most, but will always spread most effectively in good, well-drained loam; not really successful in heavy clays.
HARDINESS Hardy, tolerating at least -15°C (5°F).
SIZE About 20 x 60cm (8 x 24in) after three years; individual plants will ultimately reach about 20cm x 3-4m (8in x 10-13ft).

Camellia x williamsii 'Donation'

CARE
Mulch in autumn and early spring, and give a balanced general or rose fertilizer in spring.
PROPAGATION
By division (in the manner of a herbaceous perennial), or alternatively by layering in spring.
PRUNING
Not necessary.
PROBLEMS
None.

RECOMMENDED VARIETIES
True species only available.

Cornus canadensis

Corylopsis Winter hazel

❝ Related in name alone to the true hazels, Corylus, *the various oriental species of* Corylopsis *are members of the witch hazel family, and share their appealing late-winter-flowering habit. They really are most delightful shrubs with their almost cowslip-like, pendent, yellow scented flowers. Unfortunately, they do have an all-too-common disadvantage in being intolerant of lime. ❞*

CARE
Mulch in autumn and early spring, and give a balanced general or rose fertilizer in spring.
PROPAGATION
Easiest by layering in late summer, but also by softwood cuttings in early summer which will strike in a soil-based compost with slight warmth.
PRUNING
Not necessary.
PROBLEMS
None.

SHADE TOLERANCE Light to moderate.
SOIL Best on slightly acidic, leaf-mould-rich, moist loam. Will not tolerate alkaline conditions.
HARDINESS Hardy, tolerating at least -15°C (5°F).
SIZE About 1 x 1m (3 x 3ft) after three years, 5 x 4m (16 x 13ft) ultimately.

RECOMMENDED VARIETIES
The commonest species is *Corylopsis pauciflora* with flowers in groups of three and a fairly low growing habit, up to 2m (6ft), but *C. spicata* is an altogether taller and more floriferous plant, while *C. sinensis* 'Spring Purple' has striking purple stems that contrast delightfully with flowers and foliage.

Corylopsis pauciflora

SHRUBS

Corylus avellana Hazel

❝ Anyone who has collected wild hazelnuts from woodland will know two things – first, it is an exercise worth doing for the harvest of nuts, and second, this is a shrub that tolerates very deep shade. There are, indeed, very few shrubs that can be used as hedging in quite such shady conditions. But even if the hazelnut fruits, themselves, don't interest you, there are some appealing foliage and shoot variants and, with annual pruning, all can be kept to a manageable size. ❞

CARE

Mulch in autumn and early spring, and give a balanced general or rose fertilizer in spring.

SHADE TOLERANCE
Moderate to deep.
SOIL Almost all.
HARDINESS Very hardy, tolerating at least -20°C (-4°F).
SIZE Without pruning, about 2 x 2m (6 x 6ft) after three years, 6-8 x 6m (20-25 x 20ft) ultimately.

PROPAGATION

Easiest by removal of rooted suckers or by layering (but not with 'Contorta' which must be grafted).

PRUNING

Not essential, but an advantage to prevent the plants from becoming large and ungainly. Either coppice every four or five years by cutting down all shoots to just above soil level or, better I think, cut back the oldest third of the shoots to soil level annually, in early spring.

RECOMMENDED VARIETIES

'Contorta' is the corkscrew hazel with the twisted branches so beloved of flower arrangers, but it produces few nuts. The best foliage forms are 'Aurea' with soft-yellowish-green leaves in spring, and a variety of a related species, the filbert, *Corylus maxima* 'Purpurea', with rich purple leaves and purplish catkins. Varieties grown for nut production are generally less attractive and require rather different management.

PROBLEMS

Nut weevil can be troublesome on fruiting plants, mildew may damage foliage and other fungi may spoil nuts.

Cotoneaster

❝ There are few larger or more generally useful garden shrub genera than Cotoneaster, *with its 70 or more evergreen and deciduous species. I find it helpful to divide them into four groups for garden purposes: 1 low to medium height, deciduous; 2 low to medium height, evergreen; 3 tall, deciduous; 4 tall, evergreen. Almost all will tolerate at least light shade and I find this confers two distinct uses. Groups 3 and 4 are particularly attractive in larger woodland gardens, whereas Groups 1 and 2, which can look a trifle odd in such a semi-natural setting, are ideal for shaded courtyards and similar more formal garden settings. ❞*

SHADE TOLERANCE Light to moderate or almost deep.
SOIL Almost all.
HARDINESS Very hardy, tolerating at least -20°C (-4°F).
SIZE Group 1: slowly reaches about 1.5 x 3m (5 x 10ft) ultimately. **Group 2:** varies from about 60cm x 3m (24in x 10ft) ultimately for *C. horizontalis*, to about 1.5 x 3m (5 x 10ft) for *C. watereri* 'Pendulus'. **Group 3:** ultimately about 4 x 4m (13 x 13ft). **Group 4:** ultimately about 5-7 x 5-7 m (16-23 x 16-23ft).

CARE

Mulch in autumn and again in early spring, and give a balanced general or rose fertilizer in spring.

Cotoneaster 'Rothschildianus'

PROPAGATION

Some of the low-growing species can easily be layered but, overall, the best methods of propagation are by semi-

RECOMMENDED VARIETIES

Group 1: *Cotoneaster* 'Coral Beauty', spreading, red-pink berries, small oval greyish leaves; *C. horizontalis*, herringbone branching pattern, red berries, small leaves, good autumn colour.
Group 2: *C. dammeri*, wide spreading, good ground cover, red berries; *C. microphyllus*, tiny, glossy, dark green leaves, large red berries, forms low mound; *C. watereri* 'Pendulus' (often called 'Hybridus Pendulus'), spreading with reddish leaf stalks and bright red autumn berries, makes good ground cover.
Group 3: *C. simonsii*, white spring flowers and red berries, good as informal hedge.
Group 4: *C.* 'Rothschildianus', elongated leaves and yellow autumn berries; *C. salicifolius* 'Floccosus', elongated leaves, white beneath, red autumn berries, one of the best shrubs for covering a shaded wall.

ripe cuttings in summer or hardwood cuttings in winter, struck in soil-based compost in a cold frame. Most named forms do not come true from seed.

PRUNING

Groups 1 and 2: none necessary, other than light pruning in spring to keep to shape and size. Group 2 types can be grown as shade-tolerant hedges and should then be clipped first around mid-summer and again in early autumn.
Groups 3 and 4: none necessary, although if grown as hedges, they may be given a very light trim in spring.

PROBLEMS

None.

Daphne

" Probably more than any other plants in my garden, daphnes evoke a, 'What is producing that wonderful perfume?' response from my visitors. For while these plants are agreeable enough to look at, either in flower with their small pink or whitish blooms, or in fruit, neither deciduous nor evergreen daphnes would win many prizes for their appearance alone. But their winter or early spring fragrance is ample justification for planting them close to the edge of a woodland garden or in a small, shaded shrubbery. "

CARE

Mulch in autumn and early spring and give a balanced general or rose fertilizer in spring.

PROPAGATION

Some species, *Daphne mezereum* most notably, are more readily propagated by layering, but others will strike in a slightly humus-enriched, soil-base compost in a cold frame from semi-ripe cuttings in early summer.

SHADE TOLERANCE Light to moderate or almost deep.
SOIL Almost all.
HARDINESS Fairly to moderately hardy, tolerating -5 to -10°C (23-14°F) or slightly less.
SIZE All are fairly small and slow growing, ultimate size varying with species between about 50 x 80cm (20 x 32in) and 2 x 1m (6 x 3ft).

RECOMMENDED VARIETIES

Daphne blagayana deciduous, cream-white; *D. burkwoodii* deciduous, pink; *D. cneorum* evergreen, pink; *D. laureola* evergreen, greenish white; *D. mezereum* 'Alba' deciduous, white; *D. tangutica* evergreen dwarf, pink-purple.

PRUNING

Not necessary.

PROBLEMS

None.

Daphne tangutica

SHRUBS

Euonymus

66 Euonymus *is a genus of shrubs that I call the workhorses of the shrub garden. They are easy, reliable, relatively attractive and relatively undemanding, but never the stars of the show. Sadly, I find rather few of them more than very slightly shade tolerant, the main exception being* Euonymus fortunei, *an evergreen ground-cover species with a very wide range of leaf colours and variega-tions. Most variegated shrubs tend to lose something of the intensity of their colour in shade, but this one seldom lets me down.* 99

Euonymus fortunei 'Emerald Gaiety'

SHADE TOLERANCE Light to moderate or almost deep.
SOIL Almost all.
HARDINESS Very hardy, tolerating at least -20°C (-4°F), although very cold winds will cause some browning.
SIZE About 30 x 50cm (12 x 20in) after three years, 30-45cm x 2-3m (12-18in x 6-10ft) eventually.

CARE
Mulch in autumn and early spring. Give a balanced general fertilizer in spring.
PROPAGATION
By semi-ripe cuttings in early summer or hardwood cuttings in late autumn. Strike in sandy, soil-based compost in a cold frame.
PRUNING
Not necessary, although a neater appearance will be obtained if any long vertical shoots are cut back in spring.
PROBLEMS
None.

RECOMMENDED VARIETIES
Euonymus fortunei 'Emerald Gaiety' green and white variegation, 'Emerald 'n' Gold' pale green and yellow, 'Silver Queen' pale green leaves with white margin, 'Sunspot' probably the best of all – golden blotches on dark green leaves.

x Fatshedera lizei 'Anne Mieke'

x Fatshedera lizei

66 *This is an improbable plant, apparently the product of what was surely an unholy union between an ivy and a* Fatsia japonica. *It has a very large leaf, reminiscent of a massive green ivy but with the habit of a wide-spreading lax shrub rather than a climber. But what-ever else may be said about it, it is extremely shade tolerant and is a most valuable plant, especially in the small, 'designer' gardens cre-ated in dark inner-city courtyards. In my rural woodland, it would be like a fish out of water.* 99

SHADE TOLERANCE Moderate to deep.
SOIL Almost all.
HARDINESS Moderately hardy, tolerating about -10°C (14°F).
SIZE 1 x 1.5m (3 x 5ft) after three years, about 1.5 x 5m (5 x 16ft) ultimately.

CARE
Mulch in autumn and early spring. Give a balanced general fertilizer in spring.

PROPAGATION
Softwood cuttings in early summer, using a cold frame and a humus-rich, soil-based compost.

PRUNING
Not necessary, but misshapen branches may be cut hard back in spring.

PROBLEMS
None.

RECOMMENDED VARIETIES
Usually, only the original cross is available although there are variegated forms, of which the best is 'Variegata'.

Fatsia japonica
Castor oil plant

❝ A big plant with big leaves for very shady places. But like its bastard offspring, x Fatshedera, it is really much better in formal gardens. The leaves are very large, up to 90cm (36in) long, dark green and glossy and, although it is generally recommended as a foliage shrub, the flowers are an unexpected bonus, appearing in white clusters and hanging for a long time before eventually giving way to masses of black berries. ❞

CARE
Mulch in autumn and early spring. Give a balanced general fertilizer in spring.

PROPAGATION
Softwood cuttings in early summer, using a cold frame and a humus-rich, soil-based compost.

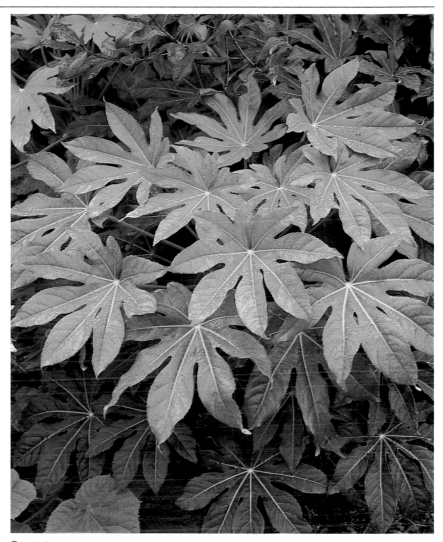

Fatsia japonica

PRUNING
Not necessary, but it may be cut back hard in spring, if necessary, and will regenerate successfully.

RECOMMENDED VARIETIES
The variegated form, 'Variegata' is an evergreen, dense bush with sprays of white flowers in autumn. It is very much less hardy and will be damaged, if not killed, by frost.

PROBLEMS
None.

SHADE TOLERANCE
Moderate to deep.
SOIL Almost all.
HARDINESS Moderately hardy, tolerating about -10°C (14°F).
SIZE 1 x 1m (3 x 3ft) after three years, about 4 x 4m (13 x 13ft) ultimately.

SHRUBS

Fothergilla major

" *Why so many gardeners struggle with witch hazels when they could grow this easier and less expensive relative must be due to the fact that, while both have fine foliage and lovely autumn colours, fothergillas lack the striking winter flowers. Their tiny white blossoms appear in early spring and are undeniably less striking, but that should not detract from the appeal of a fine, slow-growing, medium-sized plant that always looks at its best at the edge of a semi-natural woodland planting.* "

SHADE TOLERANCE Light, preferably dappled.
SOIL Moist, organic, rich and acidic; intolerant of dryness and alkalinity.
HARDINESS Very hardy, tolerating at least -20°C (-4°F).
SIZE 1 x 1m (3 x 3ft) after three years, about 4 x 4m (13 x 13ft) ultimately.

CARE
Mulch in autumn and early spring, and give a balanced general fertilizer in spring.
PROPAGATION
Most reliably by layering.
PRUNING
Not necessary.
PROBLEMS
None.

RECOMMENDED VARIETIES
Normal species only is generally available.

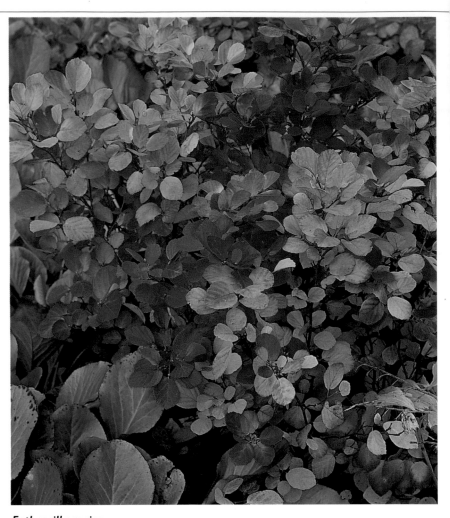

Fothergilla major

Garrya elliptica

" *This is the plant over which I risk retribution from my friends, for they know it isn't very far up my list of favourites. But there are those who appreciate its dark evergreen foliage and green winter catkins, so who am I to deny them its presence in a shady spot? In practice, I think it looks better as a wall shrub than free-standing.* "

SHADE TOLERANCE Light to moderate.
SOIL Most, although always best in a rich, well-drained loam.
HARDINESS Moderately hardy, tolerating about -10°C (14°F) although browned by cold winds.
SIZE 2 x 1m (6 x 3ft) after three years, about 5 x 4m (16 x 13ft) ultimately.

CARE

Mulch in autumn and early spring, and give a balanced general or rose fertilizer in spring.

PROPAGATION

By semi-ripe cuttings in summer, or hardwood cuttings in winter, in both cases in a cold frame.

PRUNING

Not necessary, but plants trained against a wall may be kept to shape by cutting back the previous season's shoots to about 10cm (4in) above the base immediately after flowering.

PROBLEMS

None.

RECOMMENDED VARIETIES

A form called 'James Roof', supposedly with longer catkins, is often offered but it is very variable and there is some uncertainty about how true a variety it really is.

Garrya elliptica

Gaultheria

" 'All right if you keep partridges,' was a friend's only comment when I suggested a planting of Gaultheria *under a small copse. And undoubtedly, some species of this evergreen genus of ground smothering shrubs are used as game cover. But that shouldn't detract from their value as ornamentals in shady places, too. After all, they have pretty little early-season pink or white flowers, (often pleasantly perfumed of wintergreen), rather attractive, variously-coloured fruits and year-round foliage. Partridges or not, they are plants I would gladly use in any larger shady garden that lacked chalky soil. Some species may still sometimes be found listed as* Pernettya. *"*

SHADE TOLERANCE Light to moderate.
SOIL Almost all, provided it is acidic; tolerant of considerable dryness.
HARDINESS Moderately hardy to hardy, tolerating at least -15°C (5°F).
SIZE Varies with species, but generally from about 50 x 75cm (20 x 30in) after three years, about 50cm x 3m (20in x 10ft) ultimately.

CARE

Mulch in autumn and early spring if ground cover is not too dense and give a balanced general or rose fertilizer in spring.

Gaultheria mucronata 'Stag River'

PROPAGATION

By removal of natural suckers.

PRUNING

Not necessary, but it may be clipped back as hard as required in spring, and will rejuvenate satisfactorily.

PROBLEMS

None.

RECOMMENDED VARIETIES

The commonest and most variable species is *Gaultheria mucronata*, with fruits varying from white to dark red. Among the best fruiting forms are 'Bell's Seedling' large, dark red, 'Mother of Pearl' pearly, and 'Alba' white. *G. shallon* is a vigorous species with pink-white flowers and very dark purple fruits. *G. procumbens* is less vigorous with white flowers, red fruits and very dark foliage. It is especially useful for clothing banks.

SHRUBS

Hamamelis

❝Without much fear of contradiction, I think I can say that most gardeners would place the witch hazels close to the top of a list of winter-flowering shrubs. Many would also place them close to the top of expensive and rather difficult ones too. The expense is due to the fact that they are grafted; the difficulty generally because they are grown in the wrong soil or in too exposed a spot. But in the right conditions, the combination of attractive leaves, fine autumn colour and feathery winter flowers on bare twigs adds up to a plant of genuine class. ❞

CARE
Mulch in autumn and early spring, and

SHADE TOLERANCE Light, preferably dappled.
SOIL Moist, organic, free-draining, at least neutral and preferably acidic.
HARDINESS Hardy, tolerating at least -15°C (5°F), but this is a misleading attribute because they are damaged by cold winter winds.
SIZE About 1 x 1m (3 x 3ft) after three years, up to 5-6 x 5m (16-20 x 16ft) ultimately in good conditions.·

give a balanced general or rose fertilizer in spring.

PROPAGATION
Exceedingly difficult from cuttings, which is the reason why commercial plants are grafted.

PRUNING
Not necessary, and may cause it to react adversely with shoot dieback.

RECOMMENDED VARIETIES
There are yellow-flowered forms, which I adore, and red-flowered ones, which I don't. The best yellow is *Hamamelis* x *intermedia* 'Pallida' (still often called *H. mollis* 'Pallida'), 'Hiltingbury' is good for autumn colour. The best red, if you must have it, *H.* x *i.* 'Ruby Glow'.

PROBLEMS
None.

Hydrangea

❝Everyone knows hydrangeas. At least, everyone knows the pink or blue mop-headed forms of H. macrophylla that adorn seaside gardens, but rather fewer gardeners appreciate the whole scope of this genus, of which most species have large white flower heads. The majority, including the mop-headed types, are excellent plants for the dappled light at the edge of a natural woodland or in a large shrubbery and seldom succeed or look correct in the harsher, artificial shade of a building. ❞

CARE
Mulch in autumn and early spring, and give a balanced rose fertilizer in spring.

PROPAGATION
Most species can be struck from semi-ripe cuttings taken in late summer and placed in soil-based, slightly humus-rich compost in a shaded cold frame. Plants with low hanging branches can usually be layered fairly easily.

PRUNING
Not necessary with most species, but

Hamamelis mollis 'Pallida'

SHADE TOLERANCE Light, preferably dappled for most species, although *H. quercifolia* will tolerate deep shade.
SOIL Moist, organic, free-draining, alkaline or acid, the flower colour of *H. macrophylla* varieties being reddish in the former and bluish in the latter.
HARDINESS Most are moderately hardy, tolerating -10 to -15°C (14-5°F).
SIZE Varies with species, from about 50 x 50cm (20 x 20in) to 1 x 1m (3 x 3ft) after three years, up to 1 x 1m (3 x 3ft) to 4 x 4m (13 x 13ft) ultimately.

RECOMMENDED VARIETIES

Hydrangea paniculata 'Grandiflora' elongated, fluffy white flower heads; *H. quercifolia* white flowers and huge, oak-like leaves with fine autumn colour; *H. aspera* 'Villosa' pink-lilac ray florets on exquisite lace-cap flowers; *H. macrophylla* 'Ami Pasquier' mop-head, red on alkaline, purple on acid soil, 'Blue Prince' mop-head, pink on alkaline, blue on acid soil, 'Blue Wave' lace-cap, pink on alkaline, vivid blue on acid soil.

mop-headed and lace-cap varieties of *Hydrangea macrophylla* should be pruned in mid-spring: cut out up to one-third of the oldest or weakest non-flowered shoots and cut off dead flower heads, cutting back to a strong pair of buds. *H. paniculata* should have the previous season's growth cut back in spring to within three buds of the base.

PROBLEMS
Mildew, capsid bugs.

Hydrangea quercifolia

Hypericum calycinum St John's Wort

"*There are shrubs with good reputations, there are maligned shrubs with bad reputations; and there is* Hypericum calycinum, *the Rose of Sharon. I have no difficulty in saying that this isn't a plant for every garden, or even for most gardens. It is invasive and only moderately pretty when covered with its single yellow flowers. But in a large garden and with a need for extensive evergreen ground cover in shaded conditions and even the most miserable, poor soil, it will work like nothing else will work.* "

SHADE TOLERANCE
Moderate to deep.
SOIL
Any, acid or alkaline, wet or dry.
HARDINESS Very hardy, tolerating at least -20°C (-4°C) although the foliage will brown in cold winters.
SIZE 30cm x 1m (12in x 3ft) after three years, then by suckering to 30cm x 2m (12in x 6ft).

CARE
To be honest, this plant will almost thrive on neglect, but will also benefit from a balanced general fertilizer in spring.

PROPAGATION
Easiest by removal of natural suckers.

RECOMMENDED VARIETIES
There are no named varieties worth considering. There are many species of *Hypericum*, some are very pretty and some tolerant of light shade but almost always better in sun. There is only one *H. calycinum* and nothing else will perform the same role.

PRUNING
Not necessary but may be cut back in spring as hard as desired to stimulate the development of fresh new shoot growth. Every few years trim to shape in early spring. On large areas, it can be cut back with a powered strimmer.

PROBLEMS
None.

SHRUBS

Ilex Holly

❝*In many gardens, small holly trees tend to create the shade rather than grow in it but anyone who has seen them in the wild will realise that some are, themselves, shade tolerant, their seedlings cropping up on the floor of really rather dark woodlands. There are many more species and varieties of holly than is generally appreciated, variation coming with berry colour, number of leaf spines and leaf patterning. Not all are equally reliable in shade, however, and varieties should, therefore, be chosen carefully.* ❞

SHADE TOLERANCE Light to moderate; although they grow naturally in deep shape, they then tend to lose their shape and form and hence their appeal as garden plants.
SOIL Almost any.
HARDINESS Very hardy, tolerating at least -20°C (-4°F).
SIZE Varies with species, but most are slow growing and will reach about 1m x 50cm (3ft x 20in) after three years. Thereafter, many would eventually form trees 15m (50ft) or more in height, but the leading shoot should be pruned to restrict this.

CARE
Mulch in autumn and early spring and give a balanced general or rose fertilizer in spring, at least until well established.

PROPAGATION
Ideally from semi-ripe cuttings in early summer, but they are very difficult to strike without special facilities, and the best named forms don't come true from seed.

PRUNING
Not necessary but may be clipped back as hard as required to shape and size, preferably in spring.

PROBLEMS
Leaf miner is disfiguring but harmless.

RECOMMENDED VARIETIES
Ilex altaclarensis 'Camelliifolia' few spines, purple shoots, large glossy leaves, red berries; *I. aquifolium* 'Bacciflava' yellow berries, 'Ferox Argentea' dwarf, up to 2m (6ft), very prickly leaves with white margins, no berries, 'Golden Queen' dark leaves, gold edges, no berries, 'J. C. van Tol' few spines, narrow leaves, red berries.

Juniperus Juniper

❝*Not many conifers succeed in shade; and not many conifers, strictly speaking, are shrubs. Nonetheless, among the dwarf forms of coniferous trees that have become so widely grown in recent years, none are more popular, more varied and, by and large, more useful than the junipers. And among them are a few fairly shade-tolerant, low-growing forms that I find of great ornamental merit and particularly valuable in breaking the straight line along the bottom of a tall hedge or screen.* ❞

CARE
Mulch in autumn and spring, with compost rather than animal manure. Give a balanced fertilizer in spring.

Ilex aquifolium **'Bacciflava'**

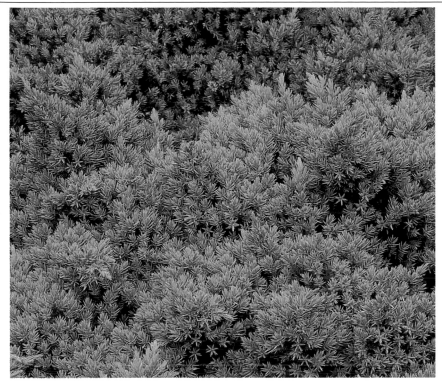

Juniperus squamata

PROPAGATION
Very difficult from cuttings without specialized facilities for maintaining a moist environment.

PRUNING
Not necessary, and although they may be trimmed lightly in spring, they will not regenerate satisfactorily after being cut back into old wood.

PROBLEMS
Red spider mites.

RECOMMENDED VARIETIES
There are almost as many dwarf, low-growing and prostrate forms of juniper as there are nurseries selling them, but my overall advice is to select the green, rather than variegated or bluish forms for shade planting.

SHADE TOLERANCE Light, to almost moderate.
SOIL Tolerates most and will survive even on fairly dry sites, but always best (and less prone to red spider mite and general needle browning), on moist, fairly rich organic loams.
HARDINESS Very hardy, tolerating at least -20°C (-4°F).
SIZE Very variable, depending on variety but do check carefully when buying as sellers often seem to underestimate ultimate size — there are some pretty big 'dwarfs' in suburban gardens. And with the various new varieties that appear each season, the ultimate size can only be guessed at.

Leucothoë

❝ *Although the North American evergreen* Leucothoë fontanesiana *has been grown in European gardens since the end of the eighteenth century, it still stimulates a 'look at the label' response when seen by most gardeners. Possibly its lack of lime tolerance explains its unfamiliarity to some, but the active promotion of a rather pretty variegated form in recent years has helped increase its popularity.* ❞

SHADE TOLERANCE Light to moderate.
SOIL Moist, humus-rich, acidic; intolerant of dryness and alkalinity.
HARDINESS Moderately hardy, tolerating about -10°C (14°F).
SIZE 1m x 60cm (3ft x 24in) after three years, 1.5 x 3-4m (5 x 10-13ft) ultimately.

CARE
Mulch in autumn and early spring. Give a balanced general fertilizer in spring.

PROPAGATION
Easiest by layering but also easy by semi-ripe cuttings in summer in a soil-based compost in a cold frame.

PRUNING
The most attractive and vigorous foliage results from cutting the oldest one-third of the shoots back to soil level every spring.

PROBLEMS
None.

RECOMMENDED VARIETIES
The form now sold almost to the exclusion of all others is the yellow and pinkish spotted 'Rainbow'.

SHRUBS

Leycesteria Himalayan honeysuckle

"For gardeners used to the 'true' Lonicera honeysuckles, leycesteria is a rather strange looking item of vegetation, but it does belong to the same family and is a close relative. It is shrubby rather than climbing, deciduous and has pendulous clusters of white flowers, each surrounded, hood-like, by rich purple bracts. It is what I call a good plant for a difficult place, the implication being that it just might not be quite good enough for a prime position. "

SHADE TOLERANCE Light to moderate.
SOIL Almost any.
HARDINESS Moderately hardy, tolerating -10 to -15°C (14-5°F).
SIZE With annual pruning, it will reach about 2 x 1m (6 x 3ft) each season when established.

CARE
Mulch in autumn and early spring, and give a balanced rose fertilizer in spring.
PROPAGATION
Not easy to strike from cuttings and variable from seed.
PRUNING
Cut down all shoots to just above soil level in early spring.
PROBLEMS
None.

RECOMMENDED VARIETIES
Normal species only is available, *Leycesteria formosa.*

Leycesteria formosa

Ligustrum Privet

"Nowadays there aren't many gardeners who plant privet; at least not the normal green-leaved form, although the golden variant makes an attractive specimen shrub. There are, however, many who have inherited privet hedges growing in inhospitable places and can't be persuaded that they could be replaced with anything more appealing. Where the inhospitality stems from deep shade and poor soil, and the requirement is for a hedge that can be close clipped, there may be some truth in this but for most situations, box, berberis, mahonia, aucuba or even laurel will probably look better. "

CARE
Should ideally be mulched in autumn and early spring, and given a balanced general fertilizer in spring.

SHADE TOLERANCE
Moderate to deep.
SOIL Almost any.
HARDINESS Very hardy, tolerating at least -20°C (-4°F) but will be browned by icy winds.
SIZE Without pruning, will reach about 1.5 x 1.5m (5 x 5ft) after three years and 6 x 6m (20 x 20ft) ultimately.

RECOMMENDED VARIETIES
The really attractive, bright form is the golden-leaved *Ligustrum ovalifolium* 'Aureum', but it is less shade tolerant. The flowers are succeeded by spherical-shaped, black fruits.

PROPAGATION
From semi-ripe cuttings in summer (use prunings) or hardwood cuttings in autumn, using a soil-based compost and cold frame.
PRUNING
Clip as frequently and hard as desired, between spring and early autumn.
PROBLEMS
Whiteflies, aphids.

Mahonia

"Mahonias offer one unusual and important feature among late-winter-flowering shrubs. For while several others are evergreen, many have yellow flowers and a number are pleasantly perfumed, hardly any have such strikingly large flower heads. But it is slightly dangerous to generalize in other respects for while the commonest, Mahonia aquifolium, the Oregon grape, is a tough customer, its relatives tend to be less hardy. "

SHADE TOLERANCE
Moderate to deep (*M. aquifolium*);
light (other forms).
SOIL Good loam for the others,
but almost any for *M. aquifolium*.
HARDINESS Hardy to very
hardy, tolerating at least -20°C
(-4°F) – rather less for 'Charity' –
but will be browned by cold winds.
SIZE *M. aquifolium* will reach
about 1 x 1m (3 x 3ft) in three
years and then spread slowly to
3m (10ft). The others are slower
growing but will ultimately reach
about 3-4 x 3m (10-13 x 10ft).

CARE
Mulch in autumn and early spring and
give a balanced rose fertilizer in spring.
PROPAGATION
From semi-ripe cuttings in summer,
using a soil-based compost in a well-
ventilated cold frame or, with *Mahonia
aquifolium*, from naturally rooted layers
or suckers.

PRUNING
Not necessary on *M. aquifolium,* unless
it is being grown as a hedge. Other
types may be left unpruned if a tall plant
is required, but they are generally better and more attractive if the non-
flowering shoots are cut back in mid-
spring by about half – at least until the
plants are well established.
PROBLEMS
Rust on *M. aquifolium*.

RECOMMENDED VARIETIES
The best form of *Mahonia
aquifolium* is 'Apollo', but it is less
invasive so less satisfactory as
ground cover and better as a specimen plant. *M. wagneri* 'Undulata' is
similar but has wavy leaves. It is
less tolerant of poor soil. The best
of the hybrids, less hardy but more
gracious, is *M. x media* 'Charity'.

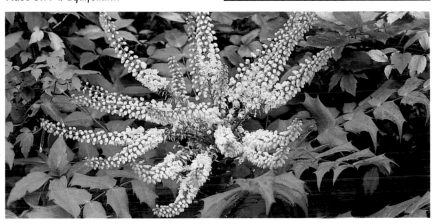

Mahonia x media 'Charity'

Osmanthus

❝ *Osmanthus is a rather
remarkable evergreen genus;
remarkable in not being grown
more extensively. It includes undemanding, pretty species which bear
very sweetly scented white flowers
at an otherwise rather scentless
time – late autumn or early spring.
Some species are fairly tender, but
those that remain would be attractive additions to any fairly natural,
lightly shaded garden.* ❞

CARE
Mulch in autumn and early spring, and
give a balanced rose fertilizer in spring.

SHADE TOLERANCE Light,
preferably dappled.
SOIL Most, provided it is not
very heavy and wet or very dry.
HARDINESS Fairly to moderately hardy, about -10°C (14°F),
but may be browned by cold
winds.
SIZE 1 x 1m (3 x 3ft) after three
years, ultimately about 4 x 4m
(13 x 13ft), although rather less
for *O. heterophyllus* 'Variegatus'.

PROPAGATION
Easiest by semi-ripe cuttings in summer, using a free-draining soil-based

RECOMMENDED VARIETIES
Osmanthus x burkwoodii particularly
fragrant white spring flowers, dark
green leaves with silvery undersides; *O. delavayi* masses of white
spring flowers, rather dull green
leaves; *O. heterophyllus* white, fragrant autumn flowers, shiny, holly-
like leaves, the form 'Variegatus' is
very attractive with white leaf
margins.

compost, in a cold frame.
PRUNING
Not necessary, but may be lightly
trimmed to shape after flowering.
PROBLEMS
None.

SHRUBS

Photinia

❝Shrubs that derive their principle interest from the colour of the young shoots are relatively unusual in gardens, but certainly shouldn't be maligned on this basis. The evergreen photinias are good examples of this, for their rich red early-spring growth is at least as appealing as many a blossom. They are easy, adaptable and relatively inexpensive and, although unlikely to win many awards on their own account, can contribute usefully to a mixed planting. ❞

SHADE TOLERANCE Light to almost moderate.
SOIL Almost any, but best on a rich organic loam and never really successful on chalky soils.
HARDINESS Moderately hardy, tolerating -10 to -15°C (14-5°F).
SIZE About 1 x 1m (3 x 3ft) after three years, 4 x 4m (13 x 13ft) ultimately.

CARE
Mulch in the autumn and early spring, and also give a balanced general fertilizer in the spring.
PROPAGATION
Semi-ripe cuttings in a rather humus-rich, soil-based compost in a cold frame in summer.
PRUNING
Not necessary, but misshapen plants will regenerate if cut back fairly hard in spring.
PROBLEMS
None.

RECOMMENDED VARIETIES
The commonest and, by and large, the best coloured plant is *Photinia fraseri* 'Red Robin' which has good winter as well as spring foliage colour.

Pieris

❝Pieris shares some features with Photinia – they are evergreen shrubs, many species being grown for their appealing shoots. But in other respects they differ: some flower well and attractively with cascades of cream-white blossom in spring and so have an additional dimension to their appeal, but unfortunately they are strictly acid soil lovers, as befits their place in the family Ericaceae. ❞

CARE
Mulch in autumn and early spring, and give a balanced rose fertilizer in spring.
PROPAGATION
Semi-ripe cuttings in a rather humus-

SHADE TOLERANCE Light to almost moderate.
SOIL Acidic, moist, humus rich, not prone to drying out.
HARDINESS Moderately hardy, tolerating about -10°C (14°F).
SIZE About 50 x 75cm (20 x 30in) after three years, 2 x 2m (6 x 6ft) ultimately.

RECOMMENDED VARIETIES
Pieris floribunda one of the best for flowers and one of the hardiest, although its shoot colour is less impressive than in the selected forms; *P.* 'Forest Flame' superbly vivid red young shoots; *P.* 'Firecrest' a good combination of flower and shoot appeal; *P. japonica* 'Purity' very long inflorescences.

rich, soil-based compost in a cold frame in summer or by layering.
PRUNING
None necessary.
PROBLEMS
None.

Pieris 'Forest Flame'

Prunus laurocerasus

Prunus laurocerasus Cherry laurel

❝ *This large-leaved evergreen laurel was the hedge plant of Victorian gardens because it was tough, it would grow almost anywhere, it tolerated urban pollution, and it was available. Today, it has largely been supplanted by more ornamental and neater species, but it retains one virtue in its shade tolerance. If you need a robust hedge for a shady place, then laurel will probably still do the job better than anything else. And one of the variegated or other ornamental forms can still make a reasonable specimen shrub.* ❞

SHADE TOLERANCE
Moderate to deep.
SOIL Almost any, but least successful on very dry sites.
HARDINESS Very hardy, tolerating at least -20°C (-4°F).
SIZE Unpruned, the normal species will reach 2 x 2m (6 x 6ft) in three years and ultimately 8-10 x 8m (26-33 x 25ft). 'Otto Luyken' will be unlikely to exceed 2 x 2m (6 x 6ft).

CARE
Mulch in autumn and early spring, and give a balanced general fertilizer in spring, at least until established.

RECOMMENDED VARIETIES
Prunus laurocerasus is ideal for hedging but, as a specimen shrub, the lower growing 'Otto Luyken' with its attractive white flowers, or 'Variegata' with cream-white leaf spots, make good choices.

PROPAGATION
Semi-ripe cuttings in a soil-based compost in a cold frame in early summer.
PRUNING
Not necessary, but when grown as a hedge, should be pruned at least once, ideally with secateurs – the large leaves tend to brown unattractively when clipped.
PROBLEMS
None.

SHRUBS

Pyracantha Firethorn

❝ *Pyracanthas have become increasingly popular in recent years, rather against the odds; the odds being fireblight disease. This serious bacterial problem affects many woody members of the rose family, and pyracanthas seem especially prone. Nonetheless, they are very attractive plants, evergreen and with appealing flowers and berries. They are also viciously thorny but, grown against a shaded wall, they make a display that few other shrubs can match.* ❞

SHADE TOLERANCE Light to moderate.
SOIL Almost any, but least successful on chalky soils.
HARDINESS Very hardy, tolerating at least -20°C (-4°F).
SIZE About 1 x 1m (3 x 3ft) after three years, 4 x 4m (13 x 13ft) ultimately.

CARE
Mulch in autumn and early spring, and give a balanced rose fertilizer in spring.

PROPAGATION
Semi-ripe cuttings in a soil-based compost in a cold frame in early summer.

PRUNING
Not necessary when grown as a free-standing specimen shrub, but for training against a wall, it should be pruned carefully and as hard as necessary in late spring, selecting branches appropriately placed to create the desired shape.

PROBLEMS
Fireblight, scab.

RECOMMENDED VARIETIES
Pyracantha coccinea 'Lalandii' orange-red berries, upright growth; *P.* 'Red Column' red berries, upright growth; *P.* 'Orange Glow' red-orange berries, upright growth; *P.* 'Teton' red berries, upright growth; *P. rogersiana* red-orange berries, rather more shade tolerant than some; *P.* 'Soleil d'Or' yellow berries, spreading habit.

Rhododendron

❝ *If ever a garden shrub could be said to need no introduction, then this is it. Even gardeners who have alkaline soil will spot a rhododendron at 50 paces and for anyone with acid soil, this is the largest and most useful group of flowering evergreens. By nature, many are woodland plants and this is worth remembering. Not only are they shade tolerant, they really thrive so much better in shade; and so much better there, too, than their close relatives the azaleas, which tend to be sun-loving.* ❞

CARE
Mulch in autumn and early spring, with an acidic mulch, such as chopped conifer needles; they don't usually respond well to animal manures. Give a balanced rose fertilizer in spring.

Rhododendron yakushimanum

SHADE TOLERANCE Light to moderate or almost deep.
SOIL Acidic, rich, organic, moist but free-draining; quite intolerant of any alkalinity.
HARDINESS Moderately hardy, tolerating -10 to -15°C (14-5°F).
SIZE Varies, (among those recommended) ultimately from about 1 x 1m (3 x 3ft) to about 3 x 2m (10 x 6ft) (see variety details).

RECOMMENDED VARIETIES

Among many hundreds of varieties, any rhododendron grower is inevitably spoiled for choice, but for most gardens the lower-growing species for smaller beds, and the hardy hybrids for planting In larger areas under trees will be the most useful. *Rhododendron impeditum* dwarf, bluish mauve; *R. williamsianum* 1m (3ft), bell-shaped, pink; *R. yakushimanum* 1m (3ft), pinkish white; *R.* 'Blue Tit' 1m (3ft), bluish mauve; *R.* 'Bow Bells' 1m (3ft), bell-shaped, pink, *R.* 'Britannia' 3m (10ft), crimson; *R.* 'Chikor' dwarf, yellow; *R.* 'Elizabeth' 1.5m (5ft), dark red.

PROPAGATION

Not easy from cuttings without specialized facilities. Many types can be successfully layered.

PRUNING

Not necessary, but where plants are small and few enough, the dead flower heads should be carefully pulled (but not cut) off.

PROBLEMS

Mildew (in some areas), leaf spotting, bud blast.

Ribes Flowering currant

❝ *Flowering currants smell of cats,' I was regularly told in my youth. I'm not sure that I agree but, in any event, this has never put me off growing them, yet another group of shrubs that I call the workhorses of the shrub garden. They are reliable, easy, cheap and really rather attractive in flower, provided you take care to choose the best named varieties. There is also one rather different and very distinguished species for a shaded site in the shape of* Ribes speciosum. ❞

Ribes odoratum

SHADE TOLERANCE Light, preferably dappled.
SOIL Almost any, although not reliable on very dry sites; *Ribes speciosum* should have richer, moist, free-draining and preferably slightly acid soil.
HARDINESS Very hardy, tolerating at least -20°C (-4°F), except *R. speciosum* which is only fairly hardy, tolerating about -5°C (23°F).
SIZE About 1 x 1m (3 x 3ft) after three years and 2.5 x 2.5m (8 x 8ft) ultimately.

CARE

Mulch in autumn and early spring, and give a balanced rose fertilizer in spring.

PROPAGATION

Strike from semi-ripe cuttings in summer, or hardwood cuttings in winter, using soil-based compost in a cold frame.

PRUNING

Cut back the oldest third of the shoots to soil level in spring each year. Old and misshapen plants will regenerate if cut back hard in spring. *Ribes speciosum* should not be pruned, other than to cut out parts damaged by frost.

PROBLEMS

Aphids.

RECOMMENDED VARIETIES

Ribes sanguineum (flowering currant): 'Album' white, 'Pulborough Scarlet' red, very long inflorescences; *Ribes odoratum* (buffalo currant) yellow, spicy perfume; *Ribes speciosum* (fuchsia-flowered gooseberry) fuchsia-like flowers, gooseberry-like leaves.

SHRUBS

Rubus Ornamental bramble

❝*As the wild bramble is so often a plant that has to be cleared from under trees when creating a woodland garden, there is some poetic justice in the fact that some of its more domesticated relatives should be planted there instead. Particularly useful is the ground smothering* Rubus tricolor *because, although the attractively stemmed forms such as* R. cock- burnianus *will thrive in such conditions, their colours are better shown off in the sun.* ❞

CARE
Mulch in autumn and early spring, and

RECOMMENDED VARIETIES

Rubus tricolor ground cover, reddish stems, bristly leaves;
R. cockburnianus white stems;
R. thibetanus brown canes with white bloom.

---

give a balanced rose fertilizer in spring.

PROPAGATION
Semi-ripe cuttings in summer, hardwood cuttings or, with ground-covering types, most easily from natural layers or suckers.

PRUNING
Ground-cover types can be clipped or strimmed back to soil level in spring if they become untidy. Ornamental-

SHADE TOLERANCE Light to deep, but best in moderate.
SOIL Almost any, although least successful on very dry sites.
HARDINESS Very hardy, tolerating -20°C (-4°F).
SIZE *R. tricolor* about 75cm x 1m (30in x 3ft) after three years, ultimately 75cm x 3-4m (30in x 10-13ft); other species 2m x 75cm (6ft x 30in) after three years, about 3 x 3m (10 x 10ft) annually when established and pruned each spring.

stemmed forms should have all stems cut back to soil level in spring.

PROBLEMS
None.

Rubus tricolor

Ruscus Butcher's broom

❝*The butcher's broom is described in most gardening books simply as 'useful'; a euphemism for 'not very attractive and it's a mystery why anyone bothers to grow it'. And, in reality, these days it is probably found more often in botany classes than gardens, because it is an undeniable oddity. It is evergreen but what appear to be the leaves are flattened stems, the true leaves being minute and scale-like. Thus, the tiny flowers seem be produced in the middle of the leaves. The sexes are on separate plants and red berries are, therefore, only produced when both are present. But whatever else is said about* Ruscus, *it grows in places where little else will.* ❞

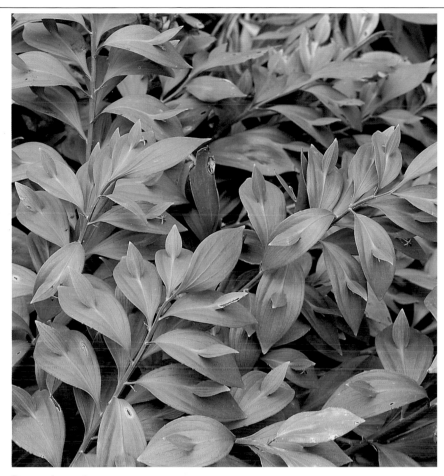

Ruscus hypoglossum

SHADE TOLERANCE
Moderate to deep.
SOIL Almost any, tolerant of dryness.
HARDINESS Very hardy, tolerating at least -20°C (-4°F).
SIZE About 50 x 50cm (20 x 20in) after three years, 1 x 1m (3 x 3ft) ultimately.

CARE
Little needed, but by mulching in autumn and early spring and giving a balanced general fertilizer in spring, you will produce butcher's broom, the like of which has seldom been seen.

PROPAGATION
By removal of natural suckers.

PRUNING
Not necessary.

PROBLEMS
None.

RECOMMENDED VARIETIES
The normal species, *Ruscus aculeatus*, is usually the one seen, and it is then a lottery to obtain both male and female plants although, from time to time, apparently hermaphrodite clones are offered.

Sambucus Elder

❝ *I have a difficulty with elders, in that I have dug out so many wild weed plants in my time that I find it hard to think of them as ornamentals. But some forms do have appealing foliage, albeit deciduous, they are quite shade tolerant and will grow in fairly poor soil. The prettiest are the golden-leaved forms and are best grown in light shade, as they scorch in full sun.* **❞**

CARE
Mulch in autumn and early spring. Give a balanced general fertilizer in spring.

PROPAGATION
By semi-ripe cuttings in summer, or hardwood cuttings in soil-based compost in a cold frame in winter.

PRUNING
The best foliage is always produced by cutting all stems back to just above soil level in spring.

PROBLEMS
Aphids.

SHADE TOLERANCE Light to moderate.
SOIL Almost any, and tolerant of considerable dryness and wetness.
HARDINESS Moderately hardy, tolerating about -10°C (14°F).
SIZE With annual pruning, will reach about 2 x 1m (6 x 3ft) each season.

RECOMMENDED VARIETIES
Sambucus racemosa 'Plumosa Aurea' golden, deeply-dissected foliage, red berries; *S. nigra* 'Aurea' golden foliage, 'Laciniata' fern-like foliage, 'Purpurea' purple foliage.

SHRUBS

Sarcococca Sweet box

❝ *A good evergreen plant for the winter garden, when the reason for its appellation 'sweet' will be apparent, for the tiny whitish flowers are imbued with a fragrance out of all proportion to their size. For the remainder of the year, its elongated leaves are just about good enough to justify it as a foliage shrub in its own right.* ❞

SHADE TOLERANCE Light to moderate.
SOIL Almost any, but always best in humus-rich, moist loam; tolerant of moderate acidity and alkalinity.
HARDINESS Hardy, tolerating about -15°C (5°F).
SIZE About 25 x 25cm (10 x 10in) after three years, 2 x 1m (6 x 3ft) ultimately.

CARE
Mulch in autumn and early spring, and give a balanced rose fertilizer in spring.
PROPAGATION
By semi-ripe cuttings in early summer in a soil-based compost in a cold frame or, more easily, by the removal of rooted suckers.
PRUNING
Not necessary.
PROBLEMS
None.

RECOMMENDED VARIETIES
Sarcococca hookeriana var. *humilis* green leaves; *S. h.* var. *digyna* purplish leaves.

Sarcococca hookeriana var. humilis

Skimmia

❝ *So many gardeners never obtain the best from their skimmias because they will insist on planting them in full sun, where the foliage yellows and the whole plant takes on an unhealthy look. There are also a good many who are attracted by the plant at the nursery and fail to appreciate its soil requirements. But given partial shade, and the correct soil, this really is a most attractive evergreen berrying shrub.* ❞

CARE
Mulch in autumn and early spring, and give a balanced rose fertilizer in spring.

SHADE TOLERANCE Light to moderate.
SOIL Acidic, moist, preferably fairly organic, intolerant of dryness and alkalinity.
HARDINESS Hardy, tolerating about -15°C (5°F).
SIZE Slow growing to about 1.5 x 1.5m (5 x 5ft) ultimately.

PROPAGATION
By semi-ripe cuttings in early summer in soil-based compost in a cold frame or, more easily, and if available, by removal of rooted suckers.
PRUNING
Not necessary.
PROBLEMS
None.

Most skimmias are unisexual and so both male and female clones will be needed to obtain the very pretty berries. *Skimmia japonica* 'Fructo Alba' female, white berries, 'Nymans' female, red berries, 'Rubella' male, very attractive red flower buds. *S. reevesiana* is fairly reliably hermaphrodite.

Stranvaesia

Stranvaesia must be the commonest garden shrub that most people have difficulty in naming. In reality, and thanks to the untiring labour of botanists, its species have now largely departed to Photinia, *but I have retained it here to avoid rendering these rather valuable plants even more elusive. They are little different from many other common woody shrubs, being semi-evergreen and bearing berries, but they do have the distinct advantage of not requiring the very best of soil conditions to provide an attractive display.*

SHADE TOLERANCE Light to moderate.
SOIL Almost any, but rather intolerant of dryness or very impoverished conditions.
HARDINESS Moderately hardy to hardy, tolerating at least -15°C (5°F).
SIZE 1.5 x 1m (5 x 3ft) after three years, about 7 x 4-5m (23 x 13-16ft) ultimately.

CARE
Mulch in autumn and early spring, and give a balanced general or rose fertilizer in spring.

PROPAGATION
By softwood cuttings in spring or even better, and generally more reliably, by layering.

PRUNING
Not necessary.

PROBLEMS
Fireblight.

The common species is *Stranvaesia (Photinia) davidiana* with red berries, but the variety 'Fructu Luteo' is a yellow-fruited form, while 'Palette' has variegated foliage.

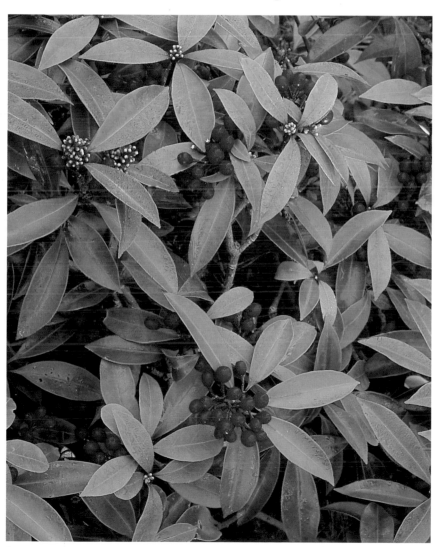

Skimmia reevesiana

SHRUBS

Symphoricarpos Snowberry

❝ *I suppose that snowberry is a good enough name, although the best varieties have large, globular pink, rather than white, fruits. Although deciduous, they do make excellent suckering, if rather tall ground-cover plants, and are especially useful on dry soils. They will also make rather loose hedges as they tolerate clipping. Their durability means that they are among the plants that best survive in neglected old cottage gardens, when most of the other cultivated vegetation has disappeared beneath the weeds.* ❞

RECOMMENDED VARIETIES

The commonest species is *Symphoricarpos rivularis* (now usually called *S. albus laevigatus*) but the various varieties of *S. x doorenbosii* are much prettier and less invasive: 'Magic Berry' pink fruits, 'Mother of Pearl' pink-pearl fruits, 'White Hedge' small white fruits.

SHADE TOLERANCE
Moderate to deep.
SOIL Almost any, including dry.
HARDINESS Very hardy, tolerating at least -20°C (-4°F).
SIZE *S. rivularis* 1 x 1m (3 x 3ft) after three years, about 2.5 x 3-4m (8 x 10-13ft) ultimately; *S. x doorenbosii* less than half this size.

CARE
Little attention is needed once established, although for best results, mulch in the autumn and early spring, and give a balanced general or rose fertilizer in the spring.

PROPAGATION
By semi-ripe cuttings in summer, hardwood cuttings in winter or by removal of natural suckers.

PRUNING
On free-standing plants, it makes sense to cut back the oldest third of the shoots to soil level in spring to maintain vigour, although the whole plant may also be cut back routinely if required. Hedges are best clipped around midsummer and again in early autumn.

PROBLEMS
None.

Taxus Yew

❝ *The yew, Taxus baccata, is another of those plants that is best known in gardens as a shade-creating tree but, in reality, has its value too as a shade-tolerant shrub or hedge. It will never tolerate as much shade as it creates, but that would be an unreasonable expectation for gardening beneath a yew is rather like gardening at night. But its tolerance of fairly dry soil and its tolerance of being clipped make it a good choice where a length of hedge must be planted beneath overhanging trees.* ❞

Symphoricarpus x *doorenbosii* 'Mother Of Pearl'

SHADE TOLERANCE Light to moderate.
SOIL Almost any, including dry.
HARDINESS Very hardy, tolerating at least -20°C (-4°F).
SIZE Ranges greatly with variety, and some forms are very slow growing but there is a popular misconception that yew hedges grow slowly too. They may be relatively slow in the early stages but within a couple of years should produce at least 30cm (12in) of new shoot growth each season, and when clipped and shaped annually, a yew hedge will attain a height of 2m (6ft) and a width of about 45cm (18in) within ten years.

RECOMMENDED VARIETIES

The normal species should be used for hedging but there are many interesting varieties for specimen purposes, none more attractive than the upright 'Fastigiata' or its coloured-leaf variants 'Fastigiata Aurea' and 'Fastigiata Aureomarginata'. Dwarf and more or less prostrate forms also occur.

CARE

Little attention needed once established, although for best results, mulch in autumn and early spring, and give a balanced general fertilizer in spring.

PROPAGATION

Best by hardwood cuttings in a cold frame in the winter.

PRUNING

As necessary; yew will tolerate hard clipping and will regenerate well when cut back into old wood.

PROBLEMS

None.

Vinca minor 'Aureovariegata Alba'

Vinca Periwinkle

" I am not alone in saying that, in my experience, there are no better ground-covering shrubs for shady sites than the vincas – the larger one for larger areas and the smaller, neater one for more limited space. In many respects, they have more in common with evergreen herbaceous perennials than shrubs and are unusually appealing in reliably producing very attractive flowers and smothering foliage. "

CARE

Little needed once established, although for best results, mulch in autumn and early spring, and give a balanced general fertilizer in spring; it can be difficult to mulch vincas satisfactorily when they are well established with soil-covering growth.

PROPAGATION

Most easily, by removal of natural layers from autumn to spring. By semi-ripe cuttings in summer, or hardwood cuttings in a cold frame in winter.

SHADE TOLERANCE Moderate to deep.
SOIL Almost any, including dry.
HARDINESS Very hardy, tolerating at least -20°C (-4°F).
SIZE Ultimate size for V. major is 50cm x 1m (20in x 3ft) and for V. minor, 20 x 80cm (8 x 32in) in about four years.

RECOMMENDED VARIETIES

Vinca major large leaves, blue flowers; *V. minor* 'Alba' white flowers, 'Atropurpurea' purple flowers, 'Aureovariegata' yellow leaf blotches, blue flowers.

PRUNING

The larger *Vinca major* is best cut back with a strimmer in spring and *V. minor*, more lightly trimmed with shears.

PROBLEMS

Rust on *V. major*; I have never seen it on *V. minor*.

PERENNIALS

Aconitum Monkshood, wolfbane

❝ *There is a decidedly sinister aura surrounding this plant, partly through its common names, partly through its undoubtedly poisonous nature, and also through the various myths and legends with which it is associated. But despite this, I think it makes a good plant, and is surely due for revival. The monk's hood of the name is an apt description of the cowled flowers in shades of blue or white. A clump or two will always look imposing at the edge of the shade garden.* ❞

SHADE TOLERANCE Light to moderate.
SOIL Moist, rich, preferably organic and well-drained, but tolerant of some clay, intolerant of poor or dry soils.
HARDINESS Very hardy, tolerating at least -20°C (-4°F).
SIZE Differs with variety; most will reach about 1.5m x 50cm (5ft x 20in) but *A. volubile* will reach 2.5m x 1.5m (8 x 5ft).

CARE

Mulch in autumn and again in early spring, and give a balanced general fertilizer in spring. Don't allow soil to dry out in summer. Thin out flower spikes in spring to leave no more than five or six per plant; cut back dead flower spikes after flowering. Most forms require no staking.

PROPAGATION

By division in spring; some forms will come true from seed sown in cool conditions in early summer in a slightly humus-rich, soil-based compost.

PROBLEMS

None.

RECOMMENDED VARIETIES

Aconitum 'Bressingham Spire' deep violet; *A. carmichaelii* 'Arendsii' deep blue flowers; *A. hemsleyanum* (also called *A. volubile*) lilac flowers, loose scrambling habit; *A.* 'Ivorine' ivory-white, bushy; *A. napellus* blue flowers, white in variety 'Albida'.

Actaea Baneberry

❝ *Like aconitums and other members of the buttercup family, actaeas are poisonous but that is no reason to shun them. The foliage always reminds me of meadowsweet, but on a smaller scale, and the flowers similarly are white and fluffy. But the main attraction lies in the autumn berries, white or red depending on the species.* ❞

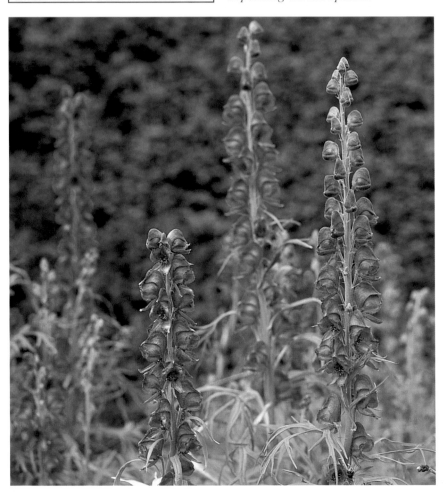

Aconitum napellus

SHADE TOLERANCE
Moderate to fairly deep.
SOIL Moist, rich, organic, quite intolerant of dryness.
HARDINESS Very hardy, tolerating at least -20°C (-4°F).
SIZE A. alba 90 x 45cm (36 x 18in); A. rubra 30 x 45cm (12 x 18in).

Actaea rubra

CARE
Mulch in autumn and early spring, and give a balanced general fertilizer in spring. It is essential to maintain soil moisture content throughout the summer. It is not necessary to cut back and they require no staking.

PROPAGATION
By division of rhizomes in spring or by fresh seed, washed free from the fleshy coating and sown in cool conditions in a humus-rich, soil-based compost.

PROBLEMS
None.

RECOMMENDED VARIETIES
Actaea alba white or slightly pinkish fruit; *A. rubra* red fruit, finely-dissected leaves.

Ajuga Bugle

❝ I confess to having problems in placing the ground-covering ajugas in the garden. They are rather too vigorous for growing among shaded rocks and paving, but not really vigorous enough to smother the soil in a truly woodland garden. I suppose that an informal shady border surrounded with other fairly vigorous species is really about right. Choose the semi-evergreen forms for year-round foliage in a range of attractive colours and bright, usually purple, dead-nettle flowers in spring. ❞

CARE
Mulch in autumn and early spring, and give a balanced general fertilizer in spring. It is very important to maintain soil moisture content throughout the summer. It is not necessary to cut back and they require no staking.

PROPAGATION
By division in spring.

PROBLEMS
None.

SHADE TOLERANCE
Moderate to fairly deep.
SOIL Most, but always better in moist, organic conditions.
HARDINESS Very hardy, tolerating at least -20°C (-4°F).
SIZE Varies slightly with variety, but most will reach about 15cm x 1m (6in x 3ft).

RECOMMENDED VARIETIES
Ajuga reptans 'Alba' whitish flowers, 'Atropurpurea' purple flowers, deep purple-bronze foliage, my favourite form, 'Multicolor' (also called 'Rainbow' or 'Tricolor') dark bronze leaves with pink, red and yellowish blotches, a bit bilious but you won't overlook it, 'Variegata' dull green leaves with cream margins, 'Burgundy Glow' red wine-coloured leaves.

Ajuga reptans 'Atropurpurea'

PERENNIALS

Alchemilla
Ladies' Mantle

❝ I know that they are deciduous and I know, therefore, that they have nothing to offer in winter but I am unrepentant in saying that alchemillas are among the top three, at least, of my choices for herbaceous ground cover in modest shade. Their foliage retains throughout the season a freshness that other plants lose with the passing of the first flush of their youth. And the billowy lime-green flower heads serve simply to enhance the delicacy and delight. To see alchemilla leaves with the drops of a summer morning dew, trapped mercury-like on their veins is to believe that all must be right with the garden. ❞

SHADE TOLERANCE Light to moderate, preferably dappled.
SOIL Most, but intolerant of very heavy wet soils.
HARDINESS Very hardy, tolerating at least -20°C (-4°F).
SIZE A. mollis will reach about 50 x 50cm (20 x 20in); A. alpina about half of this.

CARE
Mulch in late autumn after cutting back dead foliage and again in early spring, and give a balanced general fertilizer in spring. They require no staking, although the flowers may flop forward over lawn edges or paths and may temporarily need pegging back. The flower heads are best cut back when they begin to appear untidy.

PROPAGATION
By division in spring or by removing self-sown seedlings.

PROBLEMS
None.

RECOMMENDED VARIETIES
The normal species is *Alchemilla mollis*, although a very similar but rather less vigorous relative is *A. alpina*.

Anemone x hybrida
Japanese anemone

❝ There can be few plant genera of such valuable diversity as Anemone, *and for the slightly informal shady border, the Japanese anemone is its representative. Apart from its delightfully simple flowers (and so much prettier in white than pink), it has the merit of flowering late in the summer and into the autumn, just at the time when shade tolerant flowers are on the sparse side. Yes, it does have a drawback in that it can be invasive, and so should be placed with care; and the better the soil conditions, the more invasive will it become. I starve mine in a shaded gravel bed. ❞*

CARE
Mulch in autumn and early spring. Give a balanced general fertilizer in spring, if you can accommodate the vigorous growth that will ensue. Cut back dead flower heads as they fade and cut back old foliage to soil level as it browns in the winter. It requires no staking.

PROPAGATION
By division in autumn or spring.

PROBLEMS
None.

Alchemilla mollis

Anemone 'Honorine Jobert'

SHADE TOLERANCE Light to moderate.
SOIL Almost any but best in a fairly rich, well-drained soil.
HARDINESS Very hardy, tolerating at least -20°C (-4°F).
SIZE About 75 x 50-60cm (30 x 20-24in); a few varieties are slightly taller.

RECOMMENDED VARIETIES
'Honorine Jobert' white, 'Bressingham Glow' pink, but still not as good as the whites.

Aquilegia Columbine

❝ *I think I am more appreciative of the aquilegias that I acquired with my garden than of almost any other plant that it contained. They self-seed with abandon, and every spring produce charming old 'granny's bonnet' double flowers in shades of blue, mauve and pink. Yes, of course they need to be thinned out or they would take over the entire garden, but this is a small price to pay. And despite the fact that almost every other gardening book will tell you that they need a sunny position, mine look nowhere more attractive and appealing than beneath the deciduous trees of my woodland corners, which they share with hardy geraniums.* ❞

SHADE TOLERANCE Light to moderate, preferably dappled.
SOIL Almost any, but least successful in waterlogged conditions although a heavy soil alone doesn't deter them.
HARDINESS Very hardy, tolerating at least -20°C (-4°F).
SIZE About 75 x 50-60cm (30 x 20-24in).

CARE
Mulch in autumn and early spring. Give a balanced general fertilizer in spring. Pull out excess seedlings at the same time. Cut back dead flower heads as they fade and old foliage as soon as it begins to succumb to mildew. Staking is required only in windy positions.

RECOMMENDED VARIETIES
There are many species and varieties, some in assertive colours but in my experience, it is only the forms of *Aquilegia vulgaris* (often unnamed) that are really shade tolerant. The popular green and pink double-flowered 'Nora Barlow' seems an exception and is much better in the sun.

Aquilegia vulgaris

PROPAGATION
By division in autumn or spring or, easiest, by use of the self sown seedlings.
PROBLEMS
Mildew and aphids.

PERENNIALS

Aruncus Goat's beard

❝ *When, some years ago, I was asked to describe aruncus to a gardener unfamiliar with them, I offered something along the lines of, 'Rather like an astilbe but without the vulgarity'. And I don't think I would alter that notion, for in their feathery flowers, borne during the summer, divided leaves and fondness for both moisture and shade, both plants have much in common. Aruncus simply have more style, but they still probably look better in a more formal shaded garden than a woodland setting.* ❞

Aruncus dioicus

SHADE TOLERANCE Light to moderate, preferably dappled.
SOIL Moist, organic, a good plant for a shaded bog garden; quite intolerant of dryness.
HARDINESS Hardy, tolerating -15 to -20°C (5 to -4°F).
SIZE About 90 x 45cm (36 x 18in).

RECOMMENDED VARIETIES
Aruncus dioicus, the normal species, is the most impressive form although, in more limited space, the smaller 'Kneifii' may be a better choice.

CARE
Mulch in autumn and early spring, and give a balanced general fertilizer in spring. Flower heads may be cut back as they fade or can be left. They should not require staking.

PROPAGATION
By division in spring, or by sowing seed in summer or autumn in a humus-rich, soil-based compost in a cold frame.

PROBLEMS
None.

Astilbe

❝ *In view of my comments about* Aruncus, *it would only be fair if I described astilbes as like them but much more vulgar. And so it must be, for while I know that the summer-flowering astilbes have their devotees, for me they are candy-floss plants with all the subtlety of a fun fair. I have never seen a garden in which astilbes look right, for their colours and form seem to clash with everything around. And although shade tolerant, they look about as much at home under trees as do Darwin tulips.* ❞

SHADE TOLERANCE Light to moderate, preferably dappled.
SOIL Moist, organic; they are very much plants for shaded bog gardens or moist borders, intolerant of dryness.
HARDINESS Very hardy, tolerating -20°C (-4°F).
SIZE Differs with variety from about 50 x 30cm (20 x 12in) to 1.5m x 60cm (5ft x 24in), with some smaller, dwarf forms too, especially those derived from *A. simplicifolia*.

CARE

Mulch in autumn and early spring, and give a balanced general fertilizer in spring. Flower heads may be cut back as they fade or can be left. They do not normally require staking.

PROPAGATION

By division in spring; most of the garden varieties are complex hybrids that do not come true from seed.

PROBLEMS

None.

RECOMMENDED VARIETIES

There are innumerable varieties, the range of which will differ from nursery to nursery, and it ill behoves someone who dislikes the plants to tell anyone else which they should grow. But among the commoner and well-tried ones that you can expect to see fairly widely are 'Bressingham Beauty' pink,

'Fanal' red, 'Montgomery' red, 'Snowdrift' white, and a good many new German varieties, identifiable from their names, although it must be said that the range of pink-flowered forms especially is enormous, the varieties differing in colour, shade and intensity, earliness of flowering and height.

Astrantia

❝ Undervalued in general but never under appreciated by those who grow them, would perhaps be a fair summary of astrantias. Their superficially somewhat spiky flowers are much loved by flower arrangers and they certainly add interest and appeal to dull, moist corners. They are long lasting through the summer and their deeply-dissected leaves have a fresh appeal of their own as they emerge in spring. I prefer the original form with its white, if slightly green-tinged flowers, although some of the new dark reds might just usurp it in my affections. ❞

SHADE TOLERANCE Light to moderate.
SOIL Almost any, but best in a fairly rich, well-drained soil.
HARDINESS Very hardy, tolerating at least -20°C (-4°F).
SIZE About 75 x 45cm (30 x 18in).

CARE

Mulch in autumn and early spring. Give

Astrantia major

a balanced general fertilizer in spring. Leave the old flower spikes until well into the autumn, for they continue to look appealing; then cut back to soil level. It requires no staking.

PROPAGATION

By division in autumn or spring, or by seed sown in early summer in soil-based compost in a cold frame.

PROBLEMS

None.

RECOMMENDED VARIETIES

Astrantia major greenish-white flowers, 'Marjorie Fish' (also regrettably known as 'Shaggy') extra large flowers, 'Hadspen Blood' a very rich deep red.

PERENNIALS

Bergenia

Still sometimes called elephant's ears, although this is an epithet which seems singularly inappropriate to me, except in so far as both are perhaps more functional than beautiful. Certainly, if you want ground-covering, weed-suppressing growth in shade, bergenias will do it. But then, not all that many shady places are so overrun with weeds that a carpet of evergreen umbrellas is necessary. Their mainly red spring flowers can be striking at a time when much else in the garden is yellow, but I'm not sure that alone is justification for growing them. Nonetheless, I have planted plenty of bergenias in my time and, on reflection, feel that I have probably done so to give me time to think of better plants. The fact that a good many still remain must prove something.

SHADE TOLERANCE
Moderate to deep.
SOIL Almost any and tolerant of heavy clay; flowers are often better in slightly poorer soils.
HARDINESS Very hardy, tolerating at least -20°C (-4°F).
SIZE 30-45 x 30-45cm (12-18 x 12-18in).

CARE
Mulch in autumn and again in early spring, and very sparingly give a balanced general fertilizer in spring. Cut down old flower spikes as they fade. They require no staking.

PROPAGATION
By division in autumn or spring.

PROBLEMS
None.

RECOMMENDED VARIETIES
Although several species are available, most of the best garden plants are the various hybrids: 'Ballawley' rich pink flowers, shiny green leaves, 'Bressingham White' white flowers, green leaves, 'Bressingham Ruby' dark red flowers, dark green leaves that turn rich purple-red in winter. Among the species, the most valuable is *Bergenia cordifolia* in its form 'Purpurea' deep pink flowers, purple leaves.

Brunnera

Well grown, brunneras can be very pretty and live up to their unofficial name of perennial forget-me-nots, providing pretty ground cover in shade. Badly grown, they are straggly and not worth garden room. I always, therefore, give them good growing conditions and am ruthless in cutting back the old foliage. The need for good soil limits their effectiveness beneath trees and plants in woodland gardens are often enfeebled specimens. Their flowers are similar to those of forget-me-nots but their leaves larger, dull green and heart-shaped.

Brunnera macrophylla **'Dawson's White'**

SHADE TOLERANCE
Moderate to deep.
SOIL Always best in moist, rich, organic soil.
HARDINESS Very hardy, tolerating at least -20°C (-4°F) but will be browned by cold winds.
SIZE 40 × 60cm (16 × 24in).

CARE

Mulch in autumn and early spring, and give a balanced general fertilizer in spring. Trim back old flower spikes as they fade and cut off leaves browned by cold. They require no staking.

PROPAGATION

By division in autumn or spring, root cuttings in early spring, or by seed (some forms) sown in early summer in a slightly humus-rich, soil-based compost in a cold frame.

PROBLEMS

None.

Campanula
Bellflower

" There are still far too many gardeners out there who think of campanulas solely as sun lovers. But it is a big genus, all its members being readily recognisable by their mainly blue bell-shaped flowers, and among them are a few that occur naturally in woodland and are most attractively planted in comparable conditions in gardens. They need dappled light and are never really successful in the more intense shade of a wall or other artificial habitat. "

CARE

Mulch in autumn and early spring. Give a balanced general fertilizer in spring. Trim back old flower spikes as they fade and cut off leaves browned by cold. Campanulas must be staked early in the season as their stems aren't strong and soon develop kinks as they flop.

PROPAGATION

By division in autumn or spring, or by

SHADE TOLERANCE Light to moderate, dappled.
SOIL Always best in moist, rich, organic soil and intolerant of very wet, very dry or very acid soils; tolerant of alkalinity.
HARDINESS Very hardy, tolerating at least -20°C (-4°F) but evergreen foliage rosettes will be browned by cold winds.
SIZE About 80-90 × 60cm (32-36 × 24in) (*C. persicifolia* and *C. lactiflora*), about 50-60 × 30cm (20-24 × 12in) (remainder).

seed, (not for all forms) sown in early summer in a soil-based compost in a cold frame.

PROBLEMS

Slugs on young growth.

Campanula lactiflora

PERENNIALS

Cimicifuga

❝ There are plants that look right in a woodland garden and plants that don't. Cimicifugas (I can't bring myself to use their English name of bugbane) most assuredly do, their slender, almost ridiculously long, late summer, white candles of flower stems appearing far too fragile to venture in to the big harsh world outside. In reality, appearances can be deceptive, for cimicifugas aren't at all fragile. They aren't grown in enough gardens for my liking either. ❞

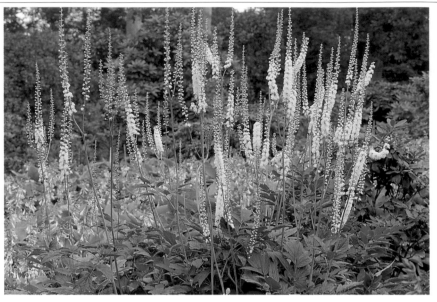

Cimicifuga racemosa

SHADE TOLERANCE Light to moderate, dappled.
SOIL Deep, rich, organic, moist.
HARDINESS Very hardy, tolerating at least -20°C (-4°F).
SIZE 2-2.5m x 60-75cm (6-8ft x 24-30in).

RECOMMENDED VARIETIES
Cimicifuga racemosa dissected leaves; *C. ramosa* 'Atropurpurea' purple leaves and stems, a lovely contrast with the white flower spikes.

CARE
Mulch in autumn and early spring, and give a balanced general fertilizer in spring. Cut down the old flower spikes as they fade. Surprisingly, they require no staking; the stems are tough and wiry and any stake would inevitably be thicker than they are.

PROPAGATION
By division in autumn or spring, or by (not for all forms) fresh seed sown in late summer in soil-based compost in a cold frame.

PROBLEMS
None.

Dicentra
Bleeding heart

❝ Dicentras remind me of fuchsias and for this reason I suppose, I always tend to think of them more as plants for the formal, sun-drenched, hanging basket-bedecked garden than the woodland habitat, their natural home. In practice, they can be planted in both formal and informal settings, although they do need the shade. But it is still difficult to reconcile those red and white, Christmas decoration flowers with anything natural. ❞

CARE
Mulch in autumn and early spring, and give a balanced general fertilizer in

SHADE TOLERANCE Light to moderate, dappled.
SOIL Deep, rich, organic, moist.
HARDINESS Very hardy, tolerating at least -20°C (-4°F).
SIZE Species about 45-60 x 45-60cm (18-24 x 18-24in); hybrids 25 x 25cm (10 x 10in).

spring. The soil must not be allowed to dry out or they will wilt and, with their brittle stems, not recover. The roots are brittle, too, so they should not be disturbed once established. Cut down the old flower spikes as they fade. It requires no staking.

PROPAGATION
Best from seed (true species) sown in early summer in soil-based compost in a propagator, with a minimum temperature of about 15°C (60°F). Other methods necessitate disturbing the plants with possible consequent loss.

PROBLEMS
None.

RECOMMENDED VARIETIES

The common pink-flowered species are *Dicentra spectabilis* and *D. formosa*, both also available as white-flowered variants called *alba*, but other good and frequently seen types are 'Luxuriant' rich pink, 'Pearl Drops' white, and 'Stuart Boothman' red-pink.

Dicentra spectabilis

Digitalis
Foxglove

" A delight that I look forward to every year in my garden is the combination of white lilies and native white Digitalis purpurea foxgloves, but I have to work to maintain the effect. For white foxgloves cannot be relied upon to come true (there are two genetic types of white foxglove; one breeds true and one doesn't). I prefer to play safe and so pink- or purple-flowered intruders are ruthlessly pulled out to keep the stock pure. All of these native plants are biennial, or, at best, short-lived perennials but there are some (slightly) longer-lived species too and these deserve a much wider audience. "

CARE
Mulch in autumn and early spring, and give a balanced general fertilizer in spring. Cut down dead flower spikes as they fade. The best way to maintain a stock of the common short-lived perennial or biennial forms is to remove and replant offsets in spring. Usually require no staking.

PROPAGATION
Best from seed sown in early summer

SHADE TOLERANCE Light to moderate or almost deep, preferably dappled.
SOIL Tolerates most, but always best in a deep, rich, organic, moist loam.
HARDINESS Very hardy, tolerating at least -20°C (-4°F).
SIZE Varies with species, from about 60 x 30cm (24 x 12in) to 2m x 50cm (6ft x 20in).

in a slightly humus-enriched, soil-based compost in a cold frame. Some forms can also be divided in spring or offsets removed for replanting. Self-sown seedlings also occur of the common native species, but where mixed-colour

RECOMMENDED VARIETIES
Digitalis purpurea very variable in shades of pink and purple and also white (see my comments left). The form sold as 'Alba' can't be relied upon to come true. There are also hybrids based on this species but most are of unpleasant mixed colours. *D. grandiflora* yellow; *D. laevigata* brown purple; *D. lanata* purple or white; *D. x mertonensis* pink; *D. parviflora* brown-purple.

populations exist, most will prove to be purple-flowered.

PROBLEMS
None.

Digitalis purpurea 'Alba'

PERENNIALS

Epimedium

❝ *I have epimediums growing close to my front door for two reasons; partly because I like them but also because my front door and the surrounding beds receive rather little sun. But I'm pleased in any event, because these are among the prettiest of smaller, more or less ever-green ground-cover plants, their foliage being especially attractive, with small, dainty and elegant sprays of flowers as an additional bonus. Do as I have done and select a range of species, and you will have an eye-catching carpet of gentle colours.* ❞

SHADE TOLERANCE Light to moderate or almost deep, preferably dappled.
SOIL Tolerates most, but always best in a deep, rich, moist loam; less successful in very dry conditions.
HARDINESS Very hardy, tolerating at least -20°C (-4°F).
SIZE Varies with species, from about 20-30 x 30cm (8-12 x 12in).

CARE
Little needed once established but, ideally, mulch in autumn and early spring, and give a balanced general fertilizer in spring. They require no staking.

PROPAGATION
Easiest by division in spring, but also by semi-ripe cuttings in late summer, or fresh seed in late summer sown in a slightly humus-enriched, soil-based-compost in a cold frame.

PROBLEMS
None.

RECOMMENDED VARIETIES
Epimedium perralderianum fresh green-bronze leaves, turning reddish-bronze, yellow flowers; *E. pubigerum* bright green leaves, pale yellow flowers; *E.* x *rubrum* green foliage, turning reddish-purple, pink and white flowers; *E.* x *warleyense* bright green leaves, orange flowers; *E.* x *youngianum* green leaves, pink flowers.

Euphorbia Spurge

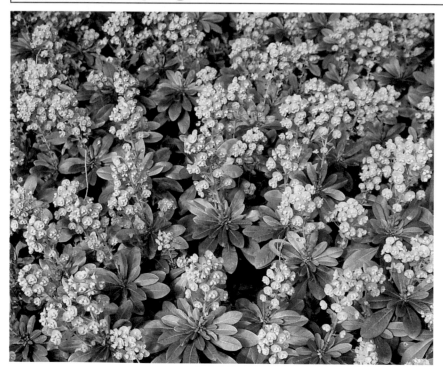

Euphorbia amygdaloides var. *robbiae*

❝ *It's always something of a miracle that euphorbias make such valuable and attractive garden plants, for a bald description of their features makes pretty dismal reading: 'flowers small and insignificant, bracts green or yellow'. But the range in the size, shape and number of the flower heads and the simple appeal of so many different shades of yellow and green make them among the most important herbaceous plants in my and many other people's gardens. It is a genus of very wide contrasts in the conditions that individual species will tolerate. Most are undeniably sun-loving, but among the remainder are a few highly shade-tolerant plants that also have that inestimable virtue of being content in dry soil.* ❞

CARE

Mulch in autumn and again in early spring, as far as practical among ground cover, and give a balanced general fertilizer in spring. Cut down the old flowering stems as they fade. From time to time it may be advantageous to use a powered strimmer on *E. robbiae* in spring to stimulate new growth. They require no staking.

PROPAGATION

By division in the autumn or spring (although not for all forms), removal of rooted runners, by fresh seed sown in the summer in a slightly humus-enriched, soil-based compost in a cold frame, by tip or basal cuttings in spring, or by semi-ripe cuttings in a soil-based compost in a shaded cold frame in the summer.

PROBLEMS

None.

SHADE TOLERANCE
Moderate to deep.
SOIL Almost any, tolerant of dry conditions.
HARDINESS Very hardy, tolerating at least -20°C (-4°F).
SIZE 30-50 x 30-50cm (12-20 x 12-20in) for individual plants, but spreads further by runners.

RECOMMENDED VARIETIES
Euphorbia amygdaloides evergreen, spreading ground cover but always manageable, greenish-yellow flowers, best in the purple-leaved form 'Rubra'; *E. a.* var. *robbiae* (still sometimes called *E. robbiae*) evergreen, rapidly spreading ground cover, yellowish-green flower heads.

Geranium macrorrhizum

Geranium
Crane's bill

❝ *On many occasions I've described* Geranium *as the most valuable genus of herbaceous perennials, and the species that are shade tolerant merely confirm their versatility. There are plants with a range of habits from prostrate ground cover to relatively tall clumps, and if geraniums do have any drawback, it is that the colour range is limited to reds, blues, purples and white, but what delicious tones there are within that span.* ❞

CARE

Mulch in autumn and again in spring, and give a balanced general fertilizer in spring. Cut down the old flowering stems as they fade. The upright forms may need light wrap-around staking but if the shade garden is sheltered, this shouldn't be necessary.

PROPAGATION

By division in autumn or spring, by seed sown in early summer in soil-based compost in a cold frame, or by lifting self-sown seedlings.

SHADE TOLERANCE Light to moderate, dappled; deep for *G. phaeum*.
SOIL Tolerates most, but always best in moist, fairly rich loams.
HARDINESS Very hardy, tolerating at least -20°C (-4°F).
SIZE 25 x 60cm (10 x 24in) for ground-cover forms; 60 x 60cm (24 x 24in) for *G. phaeum* and *G. monacense*; 60 x 90cm (24 x 36in) for *G.* 'Claridge Druce'.

RECOMMENDED VARIETIES
Geranium 'Claridge Druce' pink-lilac flowers, vigorous and invasive by self-sown seedlings; *G. monacense* 'Muldoon' purple flowers with cream and purple leaf flecking; *G. macrorrhizum* pink-purple flowers, ground cover, best spread in 'Bevan's Variety' and 'Ingwerson's Variety' but prettiest in the cream and green variegated 'Variegatum'; *G. phaeum* exquisitely dark purple flowers, there is a white-flowered form, 'Album', that is nothing like as good a plant.

PROBLEMS
None.

PERENNIALS

Haberlea

❝ Haberleas are among those plants that just look as if they should be growing on the shaded floor of a woodland, and it's a little of a mystery why they aren't planted more frequently in shaded shrubberies. They offer evergreen ground cover with short spikes of trumpet-shaped flowers in early summer. Knowing that they belong to the same family, the Gesneriaceae, as saintpaulias and streptocarpus will explain why, their flowers have a familiar look. ❞

SHADE TOLERANCE Light to moderate or almost deep.
SOIL Moist, organic, preferably rich in leaf mould.
HARDINESS Very hardy, tolerating at least -20°C (-4°F).
SIZE 15 x 30cm (6 x 12in).

CARE
Mulch in autumn and spring, as far as practical among ground cover, and give a balanced general fertilizer in spring. Do not disturb once established. Old flowering stems may be trimmed down as they fade or can be left.

PROPAGATION
By offsets in early summer, or by seed sown in summer in slightly humus-enriched, soil-based compost in a cold frame.

PROBLEMS
None.

RECOMMENDED VARIETIES
Haberlea rhodopensis violet-blue, 'Virginalis' white, and more striking in shade.

Haberlea rhodopensis

Hacquetia

❝ Hacquetias are (or strictly, hacquetia is, for there is but one species) often listed among rock garden plants. Certainly, it is small enough for the rock garden but I include it here, for the best planting I have ever seen was where it carpeted the soil, beneath a lightly-shaded shrubbery, with a mass of tiny yellow flower heads, each sitting on a ruff of bright green bracts. Certainly a very pretty and elegant thing, wherever you plant it. ❞

Hacquetia epipactis

SHADE TOLERANCE Light to moderate or almost deep.
SOIL Moist, fairly rich, organic.
HARDINESS Very hardy, tolerating at least -20°C (-4°F).
SIZE 6 x 20cm (2½ x 8in).

RECOMMENDED VARIETIES
Hacquetia epipactis is the only species.

CARE
Little needed once established, but it benefits from a light dressing of general fertilizer or bone meal in early spring.

PROPAGATION
By division in the spring, or alternatively by sowing fresh seed in early summer in humus-enriched, soil-based compost in a cold frame.

PROBLEMS
None.

Helleborus

❝ *Fashions come and go in gardening and there's no denying that, at present, hellebores are very much in favour. Nurseries specialize in them, gardening experts recommend them (I plead guilty); but with justification for they not only have uniquely attractive flowers, they also bear them for a very long time, often at otherwise bleak periods of the year, many are evergreen, most trouble free and easy to grow and, what is particularly important in the present circumstances, several are highly shade tolerant. Unfortunately they can be very variable and it is important to select named forms, wherever possible, from a specialist nursery.* ❞

CARE
Mulch in autumn and spring, and give a balanced general fertilizer in spring; cut down old foliage on evergreen forms as it discolours. It requires no staking.

PROPAGATION
By basal cuttings in spring (ideally already rooted), by division in spring (for some species; they have rhizomatous roots and don't divide easily), by seed (species) sown in early summer in soil-based compost in a cold frame or by collection of self-sown seedlings.

PROBLEMS
Leaf spotting and stem basal rot, also prone to aphid attacks in early summer.

SHADE TOLERANCE Light to moderate; deep for *H. foetidus*.
SOIL Tolerates most, but best in moist, fairly rich organic loams.
HARDINESS Very hardy, tolerating at least -20°C (-4°F).
SIZE 45-60 x 30-60cm (18-24 x 12-24in).

RECOMMENDED VARIETIES
Helleborus argutifolius (sometimes called *H. corsicus*) pale green flowers, coarsely-toothed leaves; *H. atrorubens* cup-shaped, deep-purple flowers; *H. foetidus* more or less evergreen, lime-green, purple-tipped, cup-shaped flowers; can be short-lived but perpetuates by offsets and self-sown seedlings; *H. orientalis* more or less evergreen, flowers range from white through pink and mauve to deep purple with variegated types too; they don't come true from seed so be sure to see your plant in flower before you buy it.

PERENNIALS

Hepatica

❝ Hepaticas are closely related to anemones but much less well known. This is a pity but understandable for, although notionally perennial, I find they are not very long lived – and rather like double primroses, the better the flowers, the shorter the life. They are low-growing, more or less evergreen plants with white, blue, purple or pink flowers in spring, the best, and most difficult, double. ❞

CARE
Mulch in autumn and spring, and give a balanced general fertilizer in spring. No other attention is needed and, once established, they should be disturbed as little as possible, and certainly not divided routinely.

SHADE TOLERANCE Light to moderate.
SOIL Fairly rich, moist, organic, preferably slightly alkaline.
HARDINESS Very hardy, tolerating at least -20°C (-4°F).
SIZE 15 x 20cm (6 x 8in).

RECOMMENDED VARIETIES
Hepatica nobilis flowers variable, selected forms exist and are usually simply designated by colour: 'pink form', 'blue form' and so on; *H. transsilvanica* slightly larger with blue or white flowers only.

PROPAGATION
By sowing seed in early summer in a cold frame in a soil-based compost enriched with a little leaf mould.

PROBLEMS
None.

Hepatica nobilis

x *Heucherella*

❝ After many years of growing them, I still don't know if I like heucheras. But although they are modestly shade tolerant, I can discard them here in favour of an offspring hybrid genus that is very much better. For heucherellas are the result of a cross between Heuchera and Tiarella, and it is from the latter that they obtain their value as shade plants. They bear masses of small pink flowers in early summer above a large evergreen rosette of crinkly green foliage. ❞

SHADE TOLERANCE Light to moderate or almost deep.
SOIL Most, but best in a slightly moist, organic loam.
HARDINESS Very hardy, tolerating at least -20°C (-4°F).
SIZE 35 x 30cm (14 x 12in).

CARE
Mulch in autumn and spring, and give a balanced general fertilizer in spring. Old flowering stems may be trimmed down as they fade or left as they are. They require no staking.

PROPAGATION
By division in spring; sterile so no seed is produced.

PROBLEMS
None.

RECOMMENDED VARIETIES
x *Heucherella alba* 'Bridget Bloom', bright green leaves and sprays of very small bell-shaped, rose-pink flowers in early summer; x *H. tiarelloides* ideal for ground cover.

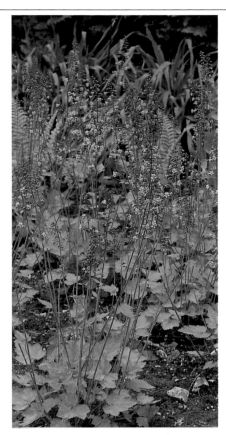

x *Heucherella alba* 'Bridget Bloom'

SHADE TOLERANCE Light to moderate or almost deep.
SOIL Most, but best in a slightly moist, organic loam.
HARDINESS Very hardy, tolerating at least -20°C (-4°F).
SIZE Differs with variety, from about 30 x 30cm (12 x 12in) to 1m x 60cm (3ft x 24in).

CARE

Mulch in autumn and spring, and give a balanced general fertilizer in spring.

Old flowering stems should be cut down as soon as they fade or they become very woody and spiky. Pull away dead leaves in late autumn. They require no staking.

PROPAGATION

By division in autumn or spring.

PROBLEMS

Slugs and snails; if they prove impossible to control, then growing the plants in containers raised slightly on 'feet' may overcome the problem. Alternatively use pellets or liquid controls.

RECOMMENDED VARIETIES

There are now so many hosta species and hybrids that it is almost impossible to give a meaningful short list, for the varieties available vary greatly from nursery to nursery. The following are those that I have grown with satisfaction: *Hosta decorata* ribbed leaves with cream-white margins; *H. fortunei* blue-green, *H. f. albopicta* yellow and green streaks; *H.* 'Francee' green with white edge; *H.* 'Gingko Craig' green with white edge; *H.* 'Krossa Regal' blue-green with wavy edge; *H. lancifolia* elongated leaves, green; *H. sieboldiana elegans* blue-green; *H.* 'Frances Williams' blue-green, yellow edges; *H. undulata marginata* (often called 'Thomas Hogg') green with cream edge.

Hosta

❝ *Hostas have been among the rising stars of the herbaceous plant world for some years, largely because of the numerous new varieties, mostly originating from North America. There are still some misconceptions about them, nonetheless: although they are primarily of foliage interest, some can be extremely pretty in flower; while generally considered plants for moist shade, many are equally happy in full sun, even in fairly dry conditions; but they remain martyrs to slugs and snails.* ❞

Hosta fortunei var. albopicta

PERENNIALS

Lamium

❝ *'Only dead-nettles' is the perception that some gardeners still have of lamiums; and I suppose with the justification that the ornamental ground-cover plants that I grow and love do belong to the same genus as the familiar waste-ground weed. And to be sure, even among the ornamental species, there are lamiums and lamiums. The worst are a little on the weedy side, but the best have some of the loveliest foliage variegation that you will see anywhere. And they do tolerate dryness which is a real added bonus.* ❞

SHADE TOLERANCE
Moderate to deep.
SOIL Most, including dry, fairly impoverished conditions.
HARDINESS Very hardy, tolerating at least -20°C (-4°F).
SIZE 15-20 x 60cm (6-8 x 24in) (*L. maculatum*); 20-30 x 30cm (8-12 x 12in) (*L. galeobdolon*).

RECOMMENDED VARIETIES
Lamium maculatum 'Aureum', is a slow-growing variety, gold leaves with white centre, pink flowers, 'Beacon Silver' very bright silvery leaves, pink flowers, 'Red Nancy' leaves silver with green edge, red flowers; *L. galeobdolon* more upright habit, yellow flowers, 'Florentinum' leaves with silver blotches, turning reddish in winter, 'Silberteppich' ('Silver Carpet') silver leaves, less spreading.

CARE
Little needed once established, but it should be given a balanced general fertilizer in spring. If the foliage persists in an attractive and healthy state, no attention is necessary but if it becomes frayed and tattered, then cut back hard in late autumn or early spring and apply a thin mulch. Some gardeners routinely remove the flowering shoots.
PROPAGATION
By division in autumn or spring, or semi-ripe cuttings in summer.
PROBLEMS
Leaf-eating beetles and similar pests.

Lamium maculatum 'Beacon Silver'

Linnaea borealis Twin-flower

❝ *Botanists should doff their hats when they encounter this plant, the only species to bear the name of the remarkable Swedish scientist, Linnaeus, who himself named and classified more plants than anyone before or since. This is a pretty, dainty little evergreen subject for a moist and shaded spot on appropriate soil. Its English name describes it perfectly for the little bell-shaped pink flowers are borne on short stalks in nodding pairs. It is sometimes described as a dwarf shrub but, although it forms a twiggy mat, to call it a shrub is really to mislead.* ❞

SHADE TOLERANCE
Moderate to deep.
SOIL Acidic, moist, organic.
HARDINESS Very hardy, tolerating at least -20°C (-4°F).
SIZE 8 x 25-30cm (3½ x 10-12in).

CARE
Little needed once established, but it should be given a balanced general fertilizer in spring.
PROPAGATION
By removal of already rooted runners in spring.
PROBLEMS
None.

RECOMMENDED VARIETIES
A variety *Linnaea borealis americana* is sometimes seen and has deeper pink flowers.

Linnaea borealis

Liriope muscari

Liriope

❝ *Almost by definition, any evergreen, fairly low-growing perennial will make useful ground cover. Liriopes come into this category, although their soil-smothering effect is achieved not through having large spreading leaves, but through having a great many very narrow ones. They have short, stout spikes of small, berry-like flowers that range in colour from white through pink and blue to mauve.* **❞**

SHADE TOLERANCE
Moderate to deep.
SOIL Almost any, including dry conditions.
HARDINESS Very hardy, tolerating at least -20°C (-4°F).
SIZE 20-30 x 30-45cm (8-12 x 12-18in).

RECOMMENDED VARIETIES
Liriope muscari spikes of thickly clustered, bell-shaped mauve-purple flowers in autumn; *L. spicata* lower growing, purple flowers in late summer, 'Alba' white flowers.

CARE
Give a balanced general fertilizer in the spring. Mulch until the plants are well established but it is impractical thereafter.
PROPAGATION
By division in spring, or by fresh seeds sown in a soil-based compost in a cold frame in late autumn.
PROBLEMS
None.

PERENNIALS

Lunaria Honesty

❝ *By no stretch of anyone's imagination is honesty a specimen plant, but it has the virtues of being easy to grow, of producing flat, silvery seedheads which are perpetually popular with flower arrangers and, above all, of flowering early in the spring. It has the merit too, as befits a native plant, of looking correct in a shrub or tree covered planting.* ❞

CARE
Little needed once established, but it will always perform better if mulched in autumn and early spring, and given a balanced general fertilizer in spring. Leave flower stems after the flowers have faded in order to benefit from the attractive seedheads.

PROPAGATION
Easiest by seed sown in early summer

SHADE TOLERANCE
Moderate to deep.
SOIL Almost any, but always best in slightly heavier, wetter soils.
HARDINESS Very hardy, tolerating at least -20°C (-4°F).
SIZE 1.2m x 30cm (4ft x 12in).

in humus-enriched, soil-based compost in a cold frame.

PROBLEMS
Most of the brassica pests and diseases, including white blister, mildew and club root can affect honesty but, in my experience, only mildew and flea beetles are ever serious.

RECOMMENDED VARIETIES
Lunaria rediviva true perennial, flowers purple; *L. annua* is a similar biennial with a range of varieties, including forms with white flowers and variegated leaves.

Lunaria annua

Lysimachia Loosestrife

❝ *Lysimachia is an interesting genus; interesting in that it is rather unexpectedly a member of the primula family, but also for its size and diversity, with around 150 species ranging from tall clump-forming species, through medium-sized, rather invasive ground-cover plants, to prostrate creeping species. They all share shade tolerance and a requirement for moist soil and, while few are good enough to play a major role in gardens, they are nonetheless pretty and useful.* ❞

SHADE TOLERANCE Light to moderate or almost deep, preferably dappled.
SOIL Moist, preferably slightly organic and rich loams.
HARDINESS Very hardy, tolerating at least -20°C (-4°F).
SIZE 90cm-1.2m x 45-60cm (36in-4ft x 18-24in) for clump forming types; 5 x 30-40cm (2 x 12-16in) or more for *L. nummularia*.

CARE
Little attention needed once established, but the clump-forming types will always perform better if mulched in autumn and early spring, and given a balanced general fertilizer in spring. The ground-cover forms, both tall and prostrate, can't effectively be mulched. Cut down flower stems on taller types after the flowers have faded. Staking is not usually required.

PROPAGATION

By division in autumn or spring, or alternatively by seed sown in early summer in humus-enriched, soil-based compost in a cold frame.

PROBLEMS

None.

RECOMMENDED VARIETIES

Lysimachia ciliata yellow flowers on leafy stems arising from basal leaf rosette; *L. clethroides* large clumps with spikes bearing masses of tiny whitish flowers in a head reminiscent of *Buddleia*; *L. ephemerum* clump forming with spikes of massed tiny white flowers; *L. nummularia* creeping Jenny, prostrate ground cover with yellow flowers, 'Aurea' is a pretty golden leaved variant although the gold turns green in deep shade; *L. punctata* yellow flowers alternating with leaves on stout stems, fairly invasive, much maligned but I find it very useful.

Mentha Mints

❝ *Herbs in general are sun loving plants but, for the shadiest part of the herb garden or for a moist shady corner on their own, mints are ideal. Indeed, on their own is really the best way to grow them for all varieties are invasive and I suggest below the way that I prefer to deal with this habit. It's a shame, however, to think of mints solely in culinary terms, for many varieties are worth growing for their distinctive aromas and attractively different foliage.* **❞**

CARE

Much the best way to grow mints is in large pots (about 20cm (8in) diameter) of soil-based compost, sunk to the rim in the soil bed. They should be lifted each autumn, any wayward shoots and runners trimmed off and the pots then replaced. Every third year, they can be renewed from cuttings.

SHADE TOLERANCE Light to moderate or almost deep.
SOIL Tolerates most, but best in rich, moist, slightly organic loams.
HARDINESS Very hardy, tolerating at least -20°C (-4°F).
SIZE Differs with variety from about 2 x 15cm (1 x 6in) for smallest creeping forms to 60cm-1m x 60cm (24in-3ft x 24in), although this spread is best limited in a container, for the most vigorous.

PROPAGATION

By division in autumn or spring or, best, by triennially taking cuttings or already rooted runners and planting them directly into fresh pots. Runners of culinary varieties may also be potted up early in the year and brought into the greenhouse for forcing. Water until well-established.

PROBLEMS

Mint rust may infect the shoots, particularly in spring.

RECOMMENDED VARIETIES

Varieties are described by reference to the aroma of the crushed foliage: *Mentha* x *gentilis* 'Variegata' ginger, dark green leaves speckled with yellow, pale mauve flowers in summer; *M. piperita* peppermint, 'Citrata' orange or eau de Cologne, 'Crispa' peppermint, curled leaves; *M. pulegium* (pennyroyal) peppermint, creeping; *M. requienii* peppermint, creeping, minute leaves; *M. spicata* spearmint, 'Moroccan' spearmint; *M. suaveolens* apple, 'Variegata' apple, variegated foliage; *M.* x *villosa* (Bowles) apple, large leaves.

Lysimachia punctata

PERENNIALS

Mimulus Monkey Flower

❝ Most mimulus like the sun and most like the wet. A few, however, are naturally plants of the woodland and are cheerful subjects for a shade garden. Indeed, cheerful is a good word to describe mimulus for they are neither grand nor commonplace, neither stately nor workaday; their colours are bright without ever really assaulting the retina. Yes, whatever else you can think to say about mimulus, they will bring some cheer to the garden and their flowers unmistakably betray them as members of the foxglove and snapdragon family. ❞

Mimulus cardinalis

SHADE TOLERANCE Light to moderate, preferably dappled.
SOIL Moist, fairly rich, organic loam.
HARDINESS Hardy, tolerating at least -15°C (5°F).
SIZE 30-60 x 30-45cm (12-24 x 12-18in).

RECOMMENDED VARIETIES
Mimulus cardinalis scarlet; *M. lewisii* rose-pink with yellow and purple markings; *M.* 'Highland Red' dark red, *M.* 'Highland Yellow' yellow, *M.* 'Malibu' orange.

CARE
Mulch in autumn and spring, and give a balanced general fertilizer in spring. The autumn mulch is especially important in cold areas to give winter protection. Cut down flowering stems as they fade; should not require staking.

PROPAGATION
By division in spring, by softwood cuttings in early summer in a humus-enriched, soil-based compost in a cold frame, or by seeds sown in early summer in a soil-based compost in a covered propagator at 15°C (60°F).

PROBLEMS
None.

Mitella

❝ Mitellas aren't plants that you trip over every day, and I count this a pity for they have an endearing, cool appearance that just looks right in a shady spot. Perhaps it is that rosette of crinkly dull green leaves that imbues them with this quality, or perhaps it is the slender spikes of small greenish-yellow flowers that appears in summer and just asks to be examined more closely. Give them a moist spot and they will self-seed contentedly. ❞

SHADE TOLERANCE Moderate to deep, preferably dappled.
SOIL Moist, fairly rich, organic loam.
HARDINESS Hardy, tolerating at least -15°C (5°F).
SIZE 15 x 15cm (6 x 6in).

CARE
Mulch lightly in the autumn and spring, and give a balanced general fertilizer in spring. Cut down flowering stems as they fade. It requires no staking.

PROPAGATION
By division in spring, or fresh seeds sown in a humus-enriched, soil-based compost in a cold frame in late summer, or by removal of self-sown seedlings.

PROBLEMS
None.

RECOMMENDED VARIETIES
Mitella breweri is the only species likely to be found.

Omphalodes

❝ Omphalodes *is a gem; almost literally, for its electric-blue flowers have a jewel-like quality that comes closer than any plant I know to emulating the appearance of a sapphire. They have been likened (by me among others) to forget-me-nots but, in truth, no forget-me-not ever had such flowers. And nor did it form neat perennial clumps of evergreen foliage (browning a little in cold winters) from which the flowers arise in such masses, mainly in spring but with a smaller crop in late summer. And to cap it all, the plant is versatile, at home in the sun as it is in dry shade.* ❞

SHADE TOLERANCE Light to moderate or almost deep.
SOIL Most, including dry sites but always better in a fairly moist, slightly humus-rich loam.
HARDINESS Very hardy, tolerating at least -20°C (-4°F), but liable to be browned by cold winds.
SIZE 25 x 30-45cm (10 x 12-18in).

CARE

Mulch lightly in autumn and in spring (although obviously this is difficult where the plant is forming a ground cover), and give a balanced general fertilizer in spring. Cut away browned foliage in early spring, but disturb as little as possible once established. It requires no staking.

PROPAGATION

By division in spring, or by basal cuttings in early summer, rooted in a humus-rich, soil-based compost. Alternatively sow seeds in pots of John Innes seed compost in spring and place in a cold frame.

PROBLEMS
None.

RECOMMENDED VARIETIES
Omphalodes cappodocica the best-coloured form; *O. verna* more usually seen but an inferior plant, the white-flowered 'Alba' is a very poor relation.

Mitella breweri

Omphalodes cappodocica

PERENNIALS

Pachysandra

❝ Pachysandra terminalis *is another of those plants that straddles the boundary between ground-creeping shrubs and herbaceous perennials. It also straddles the boundary between the good and the poor for, I confess, it is a species that has consistently disappointed me, although I know of other gardens where it forms a rather appealing carpet beneath entire woods. It has slightly elongated leaves with characteristic terminal teeth and small spikes of white flowers in spring.* ❞

CARE
Little needed once established, but give a balanced general fertilizer in the spring. Mulch individual plants until they spread to form ground cover.

PROPAGATION
By rhizome cuttings in early summer, rooted in a humus-rich, soil-based compost, or by division in spring.

PROBLEMS
None.

SHADE TOLERANCE
Moderate to deep.
SOIL Most, including dry sites, but always better in fairly moist, slightly heavy soils that don't become waterlogged.
HARDINESS Very hardy, tolerating at least -20°C (-4°F).
SIZE 20 x 30-45cm (8 x 12-18in).

RECOMMENDED VARIETIES
The normal species, *Pachysandra terminalis*, will be seen most frequently, together with the variegated foliage form, 'Variegata', which is very much slower growing and in my experience is also a great deal more reluctant to flower.

Pachysandra terminalis

Paeonia Paeony

❝ *You won't very often find paeonies recommended as plants for the shady garden. This is not surprising since the natural home of most is on sun-drenched hillsides. But I have to report my experience that, given good soil, some of them, including the singles that I love above all, thrive very well and, more importantly, look very good in light, dappled shade. For this reason, I commend them but I would steer clear of the large-flowered doubles that have a hard task managing to hold up their heads even at the best of times and with the very best of growing conditions.* ❞

SHADE TOLERANCE Light, dappled.
SOIL Moist, fairly rich, organic loam.
HARDINESS Very hardy, tolerating at least -20°C (-4°F).
SIZE 60-75 x 30-45cm (24-30 x 12-18in).

CARE
Mulch in autumn and spring, and give a balanced general fertilizer in spring. Cut down dead flower heads as soon as they fade or mould will appear on them. Cut down old foliage in autumn. They will probably require staking.

PROPAGATION
Most satisfactorily by semi-ripe cuttings in the summer, but careful division in spring is also successful, as are root cuttings in winter.

PROBLEMS
Botrytis stem blight.

Paeonia mlokosewitschii

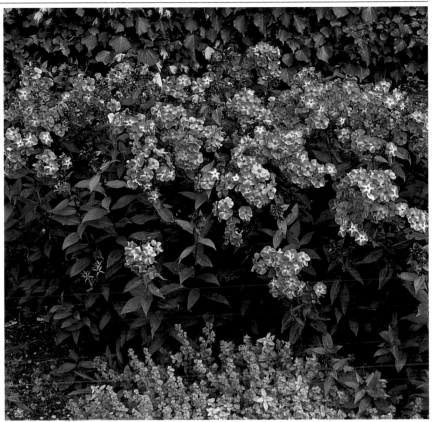

Phlox paniculata 'Eva Cullum'

Phlox

 *I suppose that much of what
I have said about paeonies could
apply to phlox – while they are in
most people's gardens, they aren't
in everyone's shade border. And I
find it is in the shadiest part of the
herbaceous or mixed border that
they are particularly valuable,
rather than in a shade garden as
such. For you will be lucky if the
whole of your border is in sun and
phlox will fill in the duller edges
with an effectiveness and shade
tolerance that few other plants of
this size and form display.* "

SHADE TOLERANCE Light,
dappled.
SOIL Moist, fairly rich, preferably
organic loam.
HARDINESS Very hardy, tolerating at least -20°C (-4°F).
SIZE 80cm-1m x 30-45cm (32in-
3ft x 12-18in).

CARE

Mulch in autumn and again in spring,
and give a balanced general fertilizer in
spring. Cut down dead flower heads
and foliage as soon as it is seriously
affected with mildew. They should not
need staking when grown in a sheltered position.

RECOMMENDED VARIETIES
Forms of *Phlox maculata*: 'Alpha'
rose pink, 'Omega' white with pink
eye; forms of *P. paniculata*: 'Border
Gem' violet, 'Eva Cullum' pink with
red eye, 'Franz Schubert' white,
'White Admiral' white.

PROPAGATION

By division in either spring or autumn,
basal cuttings in spring, semi-ripe cuttings in summer, root cuttings in winter. Cuttings are best struck in a
slightly sandy soil-based compost in a
cold frame.

PROBLEMS

Mildew and eelworm.

PERENNIALS

Podophyllum

" Most gardeners don't expect to find herbaceous perennials in the Berberis *family, but here are some to prove it, and indeed, epimediums (p.78) are other important examples. Podophyllums have big, spreading leaves, although only one or two per stem, with a few, nodding pink or white flowers, but it is their impressive, plum-like yellow or red fruits in autumn that will always attract attention and provide a good enough reason alone for growing them.* "

CARE
Mulch in autumn and spring, and give a balanced general fertilizer in spring. Cut down dead foliage in late autumn. They require no staking.

PROPAGATION
Division in spring or autumn, rhizome

SHADE TOLERANCE Light to moderate.
SOIL Moist, fairly rich and organic.
HARDINESS Very hardy, tolerating at least -20°C (-4°F).
SIZE 30-40 x 30cm (12-16 x 12in) for *P. hexandrum* or 70-80 x 30-45cm (30-32 x 12-18in) for *P. peltatum*.

RECOMMENDED VARIETIES
P. peltatum flowers white, fruit yellow; *P. hexandrum* (also called *P. emodi*) flowers pink, fruit red, sharply-toothed leaves marbled with copper-brown when young.

cuttings in early spring or by fresh seed, washed free from the fruits and sown in a slightly sandy soil-based compost in a cold frame in autumn.

PROBLEMS
None.

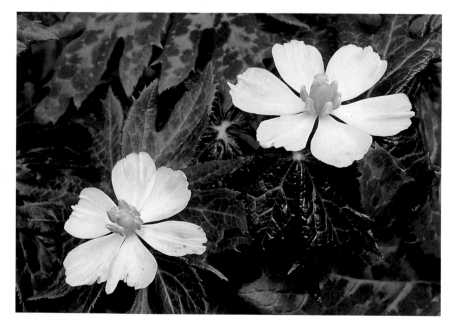

Podophyllum hexandrum

Polygonatum Solomon's Seal

" *Were it not for one factor, the various Solomon's seals would lie very close to the top of my list of interesting and valuable shade-garden plants. That factor is a small, dumpy, bee-like insect that lays eggs on the plants which subsequently hatch to produce voracious larvae that strip the leaves to a skeleton. The insect is the caterpillar-like Solomon's seal sawfly but, provided you can avoid it or control it, its host plants will grace the shadiest, dampest corner of your garden with their long, wand-like leafy stems and delightful little bell-like flowers.* "

SHADE TOLERANCE
Moderate to deep.
SOIL Tolerates most, but best in moist, fairly organic soils with plenty of leaf mould.
HARDINESS Very hardy, tolerating at least -20°C (-4°F).
SIZE 1.5-2m x 45cm (5-6ft x 18in) for *P. biflorum*; 75cm-1m x 30cm (30in-3ft x 12in) for other forms.

CARE
Mulch in autumn and spring, and give a balanced general fertilizer in spring. Cut down dead stems in autumn. They require no staking.

PROPAGATION
Division in spring or autumn.

PROBLEMS
Sawflies.

Polygonatum biflorum

Pulmonaria Lungwort

❝ *Lungwort isn't the most appetising name for a plant, but I hope that it doesn't put off potential purchasers of a valuable ground cover and one of the prettiest and most welcome signs of spring for a shady situation. The name is derived from a crude similarity between the leaf patterning and lung tissue and, in consequence, an equally crude belief that the plant would cure lung ailments. While the leaves have a coarseness of feel, there is nothing coarse about the small, predominantly blue and red flowers that I always use as a classic example to illustrate that red and blue pigments in plants are almost identical, the one changing to the other as the flowers age. Excellent for use as gound cover.* ❞

CARE

Mulch in autumn after the foliage has been cut down and, if possible, in very early spring before new growth begins. Give a balanced general fertilizer in spring. During the summer, the foliage looks pretty miserable but there is no effective way to avoid this.

PROPAGATION

Division in spring or autumn. Seeds may be sown outdoors in spring, although inferior plants may result.

PROBLEMS

None.

SHADE TOLERANCE Light to moderate, preferably dappled.
SOIL Most, provided it is moist; best results in rich fertile loam.
HARDINESS Very hardy, tolerating at least -20°C (-4°F).
SIZE 15-25 x 30-45cm (6-10 x 12-18in).

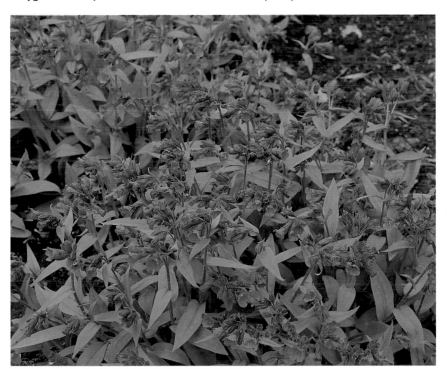

Pulmonaria angustifolia **'Munstead Blue'**

PERENNIALS

Rodgersia

  ❞ *Rodgersias are quite remarkable plants, for the appearance of their leaves is just like those of a horse-chestnut tree, although without the tree; and it is an appearance that totally belies their place in the saxifrage family. But for a fairly large and damp shaded garden, they are invaluable foliage species. The flowers are individually small but, in the best forms, occur in appealing plumes that give way to rich reddish-coloured seedheads later in the year.* **❞**

SHADE TOLERANCE
Moderate to deep, preferably dappled.
SOIL Rich, moist but well-drained, humus-rich.
HARDINESS Very hardy, tolerating at least -20°C (-4°F).
SIZE Varies with species, from 1m x 45cm (3ft x 18in) for *R. podophylla* to 1.5m x 60cm (5ft x 24in) for *R. aesculifolia*.

CARE
Mulch in autumn and spring. Give a balanced general fertilizer in spring. Never allow to dry out. Staking not necessary.

RECOMMENDED VARIETIES
Rodgersia aesculifolia white flowers; *R. pinnata* best for flower, colours ranging from white to red, and seedhead colour, 'Elegans' white flowers, 'Superba' foliage and flowers flushed pink; *R. podophylla* good bronze autumn leaf colour, 'Smaragd' cream flowers.

PROPAGATION
Division in early spring, or by seed sown fresh in autumn in a humus-enriched, soil-based compost.

PROBLEMS
None.

Rodgersia aesculifolia

Sanguinaria
Bloodroot

❝ *You don't need to be a genius to work out that* Sanguinaria *obtained its common name because its root exudes a red sap when damaged. Not that most people who grow this fine plant will ever be treated to such a display for, once planted, it is best left alone. And its flowers couldn't be in greater contrast to its sap as they are exquisitely milk-white. It is a ground-covering, but never invasive, species with lush, lobed leaves that die down without trace towards early autumn.* ❞

Sanguinaria canadensis 'Plena'

SHADE TOLERANCE
Moderate to deep, preferably dappled.
SOIL Most, but preferably moist and free-draining.
HARDINESS Very hardy, tolerating at least -20°C (-4°F).
SIZE
25 x 25-30cm (10 x 10-12in).

CARE
Mulch in autumn and very early spring with fine compost or leaf mould, and give a balanced general fertilizer in spring. Staking is not necessary.
PROPAGATION
Division in early autumn.
PROBLEMS
None.

RECOMMENDED VARIETIES
The double-flowered *Sanguinaria canadensis* 'Plena' is much the best form.

Symphytum
Comfrey

❝ *There aren't many garden plants that are better known as the ingredients of the compost heap than of the bed or border, but comfrey is one of them. In reality, the selection of long-lived, fast-growing leafy strains suitable for producing a supposedly nutrient-rich compost has tended to obscure the existence of a number of attractive, if unspectacular, coarse-leaved ground-cover forms for shady borders.* ❞

CARE
Little needed once established, but best if mulched in autumn and spring, and given a balanced general fertilizer in spring. Staking is not necessary.
PROPAGATION
Division in autumn or spring.

SHADE TOLERANCE Light.
SOIL Almost all.
HARDINESS Very hardy, tolerating at least -20°C (-4°F).
SIZE Varies from about 20 x 45-60cm (8 x 18-24in) to 60 x 60cm (24 x 24in).

RECOMMENDED VARIETIES
The hybrids are all much more attractive and generally less invasive than the species: 'Goldsmith' flowers white, pink and blue, leaves edged and splashed with cream and gold, 'Hidcote Blue' mauve-blue and white flowers, 'Hidcote Pink' pink and white flowers, 'Rubrum' deep red flowers. If you merely want to make compost, choose one of the 'Bocking' strains.

PROBLEMS
None.

PERENNIALS

Tanacetum parthenium Feverfew

" *Sufferers from migraine and people who explore hedge bottoms (the two not, of course, being mutually exclusive) will be all too familiar with this plant, for its leaves can alleviate the medical condition while the plant, as a whole, is highly tolerant of the dry, shady conditions that prevail in hedgerows. In one of its selected forms, therefore, this pretty little aromatic plant with a head of small, classic orange and white daisy flowers makes an ideal subject for a dry, shady corner, although you should be aware that it can self-seed with wicked abandon.* "

SHADE TOLERANCE Light to moderate, preferably dappled.
SOIL Most, except very wet conditions; tolerant of considerable dryness.
HARDINESS Very hardy, tolerating at least -20°C (-4°F).
SIZE 60 x 15cm (24 x 6in).

CARE
Little needed once established, but a mulch at least once a year, as well as an application of general fertilizer in spring will not go unrewarded. No staking is necessary.

PROPAGATION
By removal of self-sown seedlings or, if necessary, by sowing seed in spring in a sandy soil-based compost. Double forms are best propagated by basal cuttings in spring.

PROBLEMS
None.

RECOMMENDED VARIETIES
The normal species is pretty enough but the golden-leaved *T. parthenium* 'Aureum' is better still. Among the best fully double-flowered variants is 'White Bonnet'. 'Ball's Double White' is partially double and produces seed.

Tellima grandiflora

" *Tellimas have much in common with heucheras and I don't find them very much more attractive, for their leaves are rough, hairy things, although they do have a little more style in their greenish, somewhat understated flowers. But yet again, I am probably in the minority, for I see them in many other people's gardens, fulfilling a valuable purpose in covering otherwise bare and boring soil beneath deciduous shrubs.* "

CARE
Little needed once established, but a mulch should be applied at least once a year if the foliage fully dies down to permit this (it forms an evergreen ground cover in milder areas), and a general fertilizer should be given in spring. No staking is necessary.

PROPAGATION
By division in spring or autumn, or by sowing fresh seed in spring, in a cold frame.

PROBLEMS
None.

SHADE TOLERANCE Light to moderate or almost deep, preferably dappled.
SOIL Moist, preferably humus-rich but free-draining.
HARDINESS Very hardy, tolerating at least -20°C (-4°F).
SIZE 50 x 50cm (20 x 20in).

RECOMMENDED VARIETIES
Tellima grandiflora 'Odorata' flowers lightly scented, 'Rubra' purple foliage.

Tellima grandiflora 'Purpurea'

Thalictrum delavayi 'Hewitt's Double'

Thalictrum Meadow Rue

 6 6 *Meadow rue is perhaps a mis-leading name to give to a plant for a shady place, but a few of these tiny-flowered relatives of the but-tercups are sufficiently shade toler-ant to play a very valuable role at the back of the border or, in one instance, as woodland ground* cover. *The tallest, the varieties of* Thalictrum delavayi, *are stately things indeed with masses of purple blooms in great feathery heads, while the invasively ground-covering* T. minus *is, in my gar-den, often mistaken for a maidenhair fern.* 9 9

CARE
Mulch in autumn and spring, and give a general fertilizer in spring. Flowering stems of both border and ground-cover types should be cut back after the flowers fade. Staking of the rather fragile stems of the tall types is almost impossible and, for this reason, the plants should be placed out of the wind, in a sheltered position.

PROPAGATION
By division in spring or autumn or by fresh seed sown in soil-based compost in a cold frame in late summer.

PROBLEMS
None.

SHADE TOLERANCE Light to moderate for *T. dipterocarpum*, or almost deep for *T. minus*, prefer-ably dappled.

SOIL Tolerates most, but best in fairly moist, humus-rich conditions.

HARDINESS Very hardy, toler-ating at least -20°C (-4°F).

SIZE 1m x 30cm (3ft x 12in) for *T. dipterocarpum*, or 60 x 30cm (24 x 12in), but spreading further by runners for *T. minus*.

RECOMMENDED VARIETIES
Thalictrum delavayi 'Hewitt's Double'; *T. minus*, the species is pretty enough, but *adiantifolium* is a form selected for its fine foliage.

PERENNIALS

Tiarella
Foam flower

❝ It is only relatively recently that I've planted tiarellas in a dry shady bed at the front of my house and each time I see them, I wonder why I never did so before. 'Foam flower' is perhaps stretching fancy a bit far but, certainly, the sprays of tiny cream-white flowers have a lightness to them in early summer, and their appeal is set off by fresh green, crumpled-looking leaves. ❞

SHADE TOLERANCE
Moderate to fairly deep.
SOIL Tolerates most, including fairly dry soils.
HARDINESS Very hardy, tolerating at least -20°C (-4°F).
SIZE 15-25 x 25-45cm (6-10 x 10-18in) (*T. cordifolia* is the shorter and wider spreading).

CARE
Mulch in autumn and spring, and give a general balanced fertilizer in spring. Flowering stems may be cut back as the flowers fade although they are scarcely unsightly. Staking is not necessary.

PROPAGATION
By division in spring or autumn.

PROBLEMS
None.

RECOMMENDED VARIETIES
The commonest form, *Tiarella cordifolia* spreads rapidly and although offering useful ground cover, can become a nuisance in limited space; *T. wherryi* (also called *T. collina*) is a much better, compact plant, with leaves turning russett-coloured in autumn.

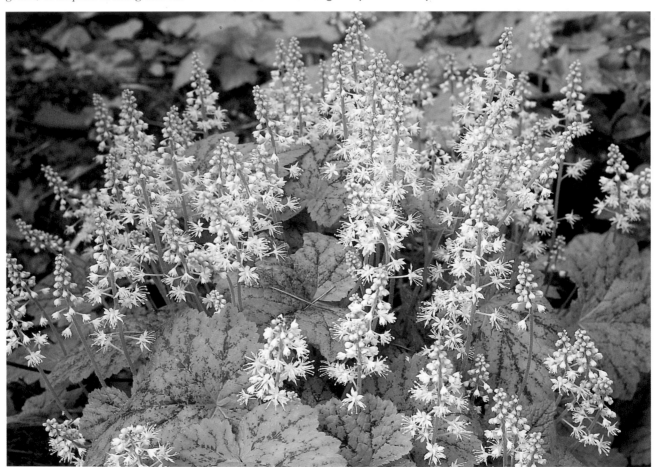

Tiarella cordifolia

Tolmeia
Piggy-back plant

❝ *This is a pretty daft name for a plant to be stuck with but I suppose any species that produces young plantlets at the base of its leaves is bound to be called piggy-back. The name shouldn't deter you from growing this member of the saxifrage family as ground cover in a cool, shady spot; and nor should the false suggestion of tenderness engendered by it being a house plant. The flowers are white and relatively insignificant but the foliage, especially in the golden variant, is rather pretty.* ❞

SHADE TOLERANCE Light to moderate, preferably dappled.
SOIL Moist, preferably organic, fairly rich.
HARDINESS Hardy, tolerating at least -15°C (5°F).
SIZE 25 x 30-45cm (10 x 12-18in).

CARE
Very little is needed once established as ground cover, but give an application of general fertilizer in spring.

PROPAGATION
By removal of baby plantlets for potting up in a humus-rich, soil-based compost.

PROBLEMS
None.

RECOMMENDED VARIETIES
The normal species is the most effective ground cover but the golden-leaved form, *Tolmeia menziesi* 'Taff's Gold', is prettier although slower growing.

Tolmeia menziesi 'Taff's Gold'

Trachystemon

❝ *Like* Symphytum, *this is another of those coarse-leaved members of the borage family with bluish flowers that have a functional, but never starring, role in the garden.* Trachystemon orientalis *will provide fairly aggressive ground cover in almost any shady spot and has, as I suppose its main virtue, a tolerance of dry soil and relative neglect.* ❞

CARE
Very little needed once established as ground cover, but it is advantageous to give an application of general balanced

SHADE TOLERANCE Light to moderate or almost deep.
SOIL Most, including dry sites.
HARDINESS Very hardy, tolerating at least -20°C (-4°F).
SIZE 40-50 x 60-75cm (16-20 x 24-30in).

RECOMMENDED VARIETIES
The normal species, *Trachystemon orientalis*, is the only one available.

fertilizer in the spring. Mulch in the autumn until successfully established.

PROPAGATION
By division in spring or autumn.

PROBLEMS
None.

PERENNIALS

Uvularia
Merry bells

❝ *Strictly, uvularias should be placed with their bulbous relatives in the lily family but they produce rhizomes instead, and have much more in common with more conventional herbaceous perennials and another plant with the same affinities,* Polygonatum. *Like Solomon's seals, they have arching stems, but are most attractively bedecked in spring with golden yellow bell-like flowers. They are perhaps one of the more surprisingly neglected of shade-garden groups.* ❞

Uvularia grandiflora

SHADE TOLERANCE
Moderate to deep.
SOIL Moist, preferably organic and rich but well-drained.
HARDINESS Very hardy, tolerating at least -20°C (-4°F).
SIZE 60 x 25cm (24 x 10in).

CARE
Mulch in autumn and spring, and give a general fertilizer in spring. Cut down old flower stems in autumn.

PROPAGATION
By division in spring, or by sowing fresh seed in a humus-enriched, soil-based compost in a cold frame in autumn.

PROBLEMS
None.

> **RECOMMENDED VARIETIES**
> *Uvularia grandiflora* is the most common and best species.

Vancouveria

❝ *Vancouverias are closely related to epimediums, and are equally unexpected as members of the berberis family. They are, indeed, almost scaled down versions of epimediums with lower growth and with rather finely-divided leaves, somewhat reminiscent of* Thalictrum minus. *They are among the plants that I came to unexpectedly late in my gardening career and have endeavoured since to ensure that others know of them sooner.* ❞

CARE
Mulch with fairly fine compost or leaf mould in autumn and spring. Give a general fertilizer in spring.

Vancouveria hexandra

PROPAGATION
By division in spring or by sowing fresh seed in a humus-enriched, soil-based compost in a cold frame in autumn.

PROBLEMS
None.

SHADE TOLERANCE Light to moderate or almost deep, preferably dappled.
SOIL Tolerates most, provided it is not very dry but best in a fairly rich organic loam.
HARDINESS Hardy, tolerating at least -15°C (5°F).
SIZE 15 x 25cm (6 x 10in).

> **RECOMMENDED VARIETIES**
> *Vancouveria hexandra* sprays of many tiny white flowers.

Veratrum

❝ Veratrum *is another genus from the lily family that has deserted its bulbous companions in favour of creeping rhizomes. They are uniquely special among woodland plants, however, in their combination of large size, curiously pleated leaves and, in the most common and desirable species, dark purple, almost black flowers. Although I have found them to thrive in fairly deep shade, the flower spikes are so dark that they then tend almost to disappear from view, and, therefore, they are much better when interplanted with paler-coloured things at a woodland edge.* ❞

SHADE TOLERANCE Light to moderate, dappled.
SOIL Moist, well-drained, fairly organic.
HARDINESS Very hardy, tolerating at least -20°C (-4°F).
SIZE 2m x 60-75cm (6ft x 24-30in).

RECOMMENDED VARIETIES
Veratrum nigrum is the only species normally available.

CARE
Mulch in the autumn and spring. Apply a general fertilizer in spring. Staking is not necessary if grown in a sheltered spot. Cut down flower stems as the blooms fade.

PROPAGATION
By division in spring, but should only be done when essential, as mature plants resent disturbance. Fresh seed may be sown in autumn in a soil-based compost in a cold frame. Germination is erratic and subsequent growth is slow. Plants may take three years to flower.

PROBLEMS
None.

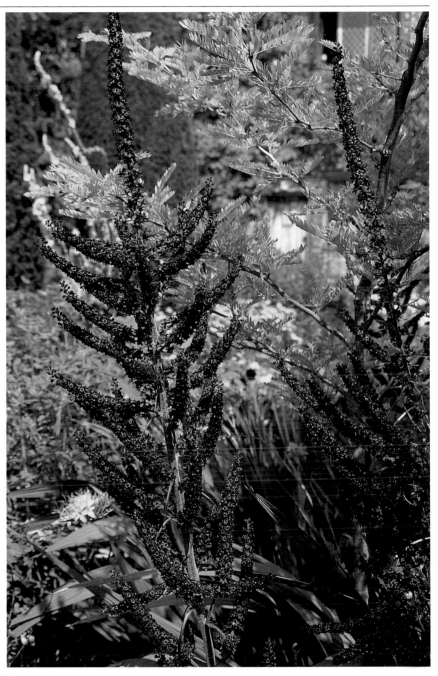

Veratrum nigrum

PERENNIALS

Veronica
Speedwell

❝ *You only need to look closely at an individual flower to recognise a veronica, even though most of the ornamental garden types have them massed together in spike-like inflorescences. And in most instances, you will find yourself making the examination in full sun but there are, nonetheless, a few species that I have found will thrive and enliven lightly shady places with their delicious shades of blue or white. The tall, slender* Veronica virginica *(now often called* Veronicastrum virginicum*) is the best among them, along with selected forms of* V. longifolia. ❞

SHADE TOLERANCE Light, preferably dappled.
SOIL Tolerates most, but best in slightly moist, rich loams.
HARDINESS Very hardy, tolerating at least -20°C (-4°F).
SIZE 90cm-1.5m x 30cm (36in-5ft x 12in).

CARE
Mulch in autumn and spring, and give a general fertilizer in spring. Stake early before the stems begin to kink, particularly in exposed sites, and cut down dead flower heads as the blooms fade.

PROPAGATION
By division in spring or autumn, or by removal of basal rooted shoots in early autumn for planting in a soil-based compost in a cold frame.

PROBLEMS
Mildew.

Veronica longifolia **'Icicle'**

Viola

❝ *Violas in one form or another are to be found in most gardens and tolerate a wide range of conditions. Some are annual and some perennial but with very, very few exceptions, shade tolerance isn't one of their virtues. The exception is a small group of species, among which the North American* Viola labradorica *is the most familiar. As befits a plant from so far north, it is exceptionally hardy and will produce its tiny purple flowers in really rather dark and inhospitable places. It must, however, have some moisture and sadly, my dry shade border proved its undoing. ❞

CARE
Mulch very lightly in autumn until well established as ground cover. Apply general fertilizer in spring.

Viola labradorica **'Purpurea'**

PROPAGATION

By division in spring or autumn, or by removal of rooted creeping stems.

PROBLEMS

Mildew.

SHADE TOLERANCE
Moderate to deep.
SOIL Tolerates most, except dry sites and always best in rich, moist organic loam.
HARDINESS Very hardy, tolerating at least -20°C (-4°F).
SIZE 5 x 30cm (2 x 12in).

RECOMMENDED VARIETIES
Viola labradorica 'Purpurea' has attractive deep greenish-purple foliage.

Waldsteinia

66 Despite their name, which conjures up an image of a Gothic horror story, waldsteinias are rather like yellow-flowered strawberries and belong, with the true strawberries, in the rose family. They make very good, closely-growing ground cover for moist woodland gardens; but sadly don't produce a crop of yellow strawberries. They are particularly effective where they can be planted over a fairly small area because, once established as an extensive ground-covering foliage carpet, the potential for producing flowers seems to decline. 99

CARE

Mulch in autumn, at least until well established as ground cover. Apply general fertilizer in spring.

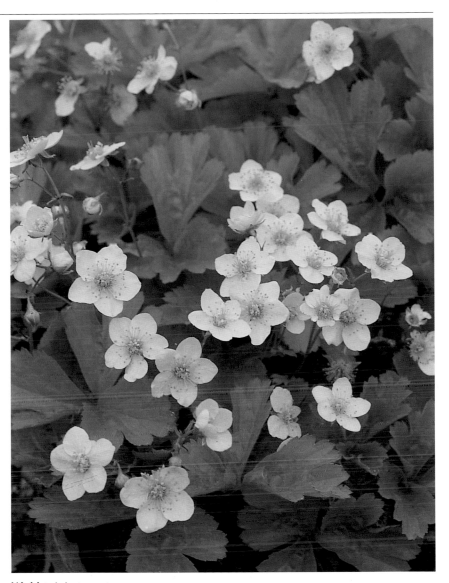

Waldsteinia ternata

PROPAGATION

By division in spring or autumn, or by rooted shoots.

PROBLEMS

None.

RECOMMENDED VARIETIES
Waldsteinia ternata is the only species normally available.

SHADE TOLERANCE
Moderate to deep, preferably dappled.
SOIL Moist, well-drained, fairly organic.
HARDINESS Very hardy, tolerating at least -20°C (-4°F).
SIZE 10 x 30-45cm (4 x 12-18in).

FERNS

If one group of plants can be said to exemplify gardening in shady places, that group must be the ferns. But, in bald terms, all the odds seem stacked against them: no flowers, all more or less green (and with not even much variation in its shade), many of them deciduous with nothing to show at all in winter, many with long names that are extremely difficult to remember, and most types very difficult to identify. It is a dispiriting catalogue. But against all of this must be set their tolerance (and indeed, in most instances, requirement) of shade and damp, a delicacy and individuality of form quite unlike any other type of plant, a wide range of size and vigour, ease of cultivation, lack of pest and disease problems, minimal need for care and attention and, now, I am pleased to say, relative ease of supply. And to cap it all, there is the fascination of knowing that this is a group of plants that has populated the earth in much the same form since before the dinosaurs. I love them to the extent that not only do ferns occupy all of the damp and shady spots in my garden, but I have a special bed for them too.

CARE

Little attention needed once established, but it is important (with very few exceptions) that they are not allowed to dry out for long periods. Ideally therefore, they should be mulched in autumn and spring, and given a light dressing of bone meal or a general fertilizer in early spring. I always use compost or other plant-derived matter for mulching, having found that ferns respond much less satisfactorily to animal manures. With deciduous types, the dead fronds should be cut down in late autumn or, with the more tender species, in early spring. Evergreen forms may be left to their own devices although they tend, after some years, to form a rather untidy mound and I now prefer to cut down all of the old fronds in spring, choosing a time when the worst of the frosts are over but before the 'crooks' (the brittle new shoots) have begun to unfurl and would easily be damaged. Fern fronds should always be cut and not pulled for the crown on small

Athyrium nipponium **'Pictum'**

FERNS FROM SPORES

In gardens, some species of fern will reproduce naturally and young plants will frequently be found; the hart's tongue fern, *Asplenium scolopendrium* does this reliably and, in general, the more undisturbed the habitat, the more likely are young plants to occur. Unfortunately, the activities of cultivation – mulching, forking and other disturbances of the soil mean that fern reproduction is not as reliable in gardens as in the wild.

It is sometimes possible to buy packets of fern spores, although the best source of them is a mature parent plant, but it is worth remembering that some of the most attractive fern foliage variants are sterile and can only be propagated vegetatively.

WHAT TO LOOK FOR

The spores are produced in small bodies, called sori, which are borne on the undersides of the mature fronds. It is the variation in colour, size and patterning of the sori that adds to the attractiveness of the fronds and is also an aid to identification. When mature (the timing of which will vary with species from late spring through to the autumn), the sori are usually dark brown or black and if they are examined with a small magnifying lens, it is possible to see if any of the dust-like spores are being discharged.

OBTAINING SPORES

Cut off a clean frond bearing ripe spores and fold it in a sheet of dry white paper, making a simple envelope, and place this somewhere cool, dry and well ventilated for about a week. By then, the spores should have been shed and will appear like brown dust. Use a small paint brush to dust away any contaminating debris and tip the spores into a small paper packet; most types will remain viable for a year or more if kept in a fridge.

It is most important to keep the spore-sowing medium as free as possible from contaminating spores of other organisms, such as fungi and algae, which will rapidly swamp the tiny fern prothalli. Nonetheless, I have very successfully produced ferns from spores without going to the trouble of disinfecting the material at every stage, as is frequently suggested.

PREPARING THE GROWING MEDIUM

I use clay plant pots with the drainage holes mostly covered or, even better, seed pans, (provided they have some drainage), filled with a finely-sieved mixture of equal parts by volume of (preferably unfertilized) garden loam and leaf mould. The surface is carefully firmed and a sheet of glass laid over the top. I then place the pot and cover in a microwave oven at full setting for about five minutes to sterilize the mixture, but an alternative method is to pour boiling water over it, soak the glass in boiling water and then replace it on top and allow the pot to drain.

SOWING THE SPORES

Once the compost has cooled, the spores should be added, preferably inside the house rather than in the greenhouse, where contaminating organisms are more likely to be blown in. Gently scatter the spores, as thinly as possible, over the surface and then replace the glass. The pot with its cover should then be placed in a cool damp place for several weeks. At first, a green film-like growth of prothalli should be expected, followed by tiny fronds some weeks later but the glass cover must not be removed until fronds do appear. As they become recognisable young plants, they should be pricked on to pots of compost, covered at first to keep them damp and then grown on in the same way as conventional plants for about 12 months before planting out.

species is easily damaged, while on large types, the tough sharp stems can cut the fingers.

PROPAGATION

Almost all ferns can be divided successfully in spring, but don't be tempted to do this with very small and young plants. Take care to replant to the same depth as that in which the parent was growing, being especially careful not to bury surface-rooting rhizomes. Many ferns can also be propagated successfully from spores (see Box), but it is a fairly slow process and it should be realised that spores don't grow directly into a recognisable fern plant but develop, instead, into a tiny, sexually reproducing body, called a prothallus, which is very delicate and will easily dry out and die. It is from this prothallus that the fern plant proper arises.

PROBLEMS

None.

FERNS

Adiantum
Maidenhair ferns

❝ *If there is one type of fern that is more likely to be recognised by the non-expert, it must be the maidenhairs for they have an individuality in the apparent delicacy and structure of their fronds that sets them apart. The wiry rachis (frond stalk) typically has single rows of more or less rounded pinnae along each side, often close together so they overlap in a tile-like fashion. But it is worth saying that this delicacy is misleading for the rachis is tough and much less likely to be broken than that of many a stouter looking plant. The following varieties are all deciduous.* ❞

SHADE TOLERANCE Light to moderate.
SOIL Moist, well-drained, fairly organic.
HARDINESS Very hardy, tolerating at least -20°C (-4°F).
SIZE Varies with species, 15-20cm (6-8in) for *A. venustum* and *A. p. subpumilum*, 45cm (18in) for *A. pedatum*.

RECOMMENDED VARIETIES
Adiantum pedatum rachis branched, so overall frond appears like a bird's foot, toothed pinnae, *A. p. subpumilum* (also called *aleuticum*) compact habit so pinnae closely overlap; *A. venustum* low growing, spreading, fronds more or less triangular and pale green.

Asplenium

❝ *In common with most people, I suppose, it was a species of* Asplenium *that was the first fern I could identify, and even today it remains the easiest (although to be honest,* A. scolopendrium, *the hart's tongue fern, in common with many other ferns, has flitted from genus to genus over the years). Although the group is very large, relatively few species are hardy, but all are evergreen and most of the good garden forms are characterized by beautifully fresh, almost undivided fronds, and are tolerant of a wide range of soils. Most usefully, some are highly lime tolerant and are much at home in the crevices of limestone walls or growing among mortar. In my own fern bed, it is varieties of* Asplenium *that self-seed most freely in the cracks of the old brick wall alongside.* ❞

RECOMMENDED VARIETIES
Asplenium scolopendrium (still sometimes called *Scolopendrium vulgare*) (hart's tongue fern) strap-like undivided fronds, many variants exist, all smaller in size than the true species and of which the best are 'Undulatum' (wavy margins), the 'Cristatum' group (divided tips or crests to the fronds) and 'Kaye's Lacerated' (torn or frayed margins); *A. ceterach* (often called *Ceterach officinarum*) (rusty back fern) lobed fronds with dense pale brown scales beneath.

Adiantum pedatum

SHADE TOLERANCE

A. scolopendrium, light to deep; *A. ceterach*, light.

SOIL *A. scolopendrium*, generally most luxuriant in moist, well-drained, fairly organic and rich soils but tolerant of dry, impoverished positions too. *A. ceterach*, fairly dry, alkaline.

HARDINESS Very hardy, tolerating at least -20°C (-4°F).

SIZE 90 x 60cm (36 x 24in) for *A. scolopendrium*, 20 x 10cm (8 x 4in) for *A. ceterach*.

Athyrium nipponicum 'Pictum'

Athyrium

" Although Athyrium is a big genus, its garden merits rest on very few species, and most notably on the lady fern, Athyrium filix-femina, a 'typical' native fern with deeply-dissected fronds, but which has given rise to a prodigious number of varieties. They are almost all very easy and undemanding plants but there is a big range in size among the selected forms which must, therefore, be chosen carefully. "

SHADE TOLERANCE Light to moderate, preferably dappled.

SOIL Moist, well-drained, fairly organic, preferably leaf mould rich and slightly, but not essentially, acid.

HARDINESS Very hardy, tolerating at least -20°C (-4°F) but needs shelter from cold winds.

SIZE Varies widely with species, from 20 x 10-15cm (8 x 4-6in) to 1m x 60cm (3ft x 24in) (see right).

RECOMMENDED VARIETIES

Athyrium filix-femina (lady fern) 1m x 60cm (3ft x 24in) deeply-dissected, lace-like deciduous fronds, 'Corymbiferum' crested fronds with a congested terminal tassel, 'Frizelliae' 20 x 10-15cm (8 x 4-6in), pinnae on fronds take form of congested knots, 'Minutissimum' 20 x 20cm (8 x 8in), scaled-down version of the species, 'Plumosum' group 1m x 60cm (3ft x 24in), broad, more or less golden-green fronds of very delicate appearance, 'Victoriae' 45cm x 1m (18in x 3ft), pinnae and pinnules divided to form appearance of crosses, exquisitely lovely but the true form is now very rarely seen; only buy plants under this name from specialist expert fern nurseries or you are likely to be disappointed. *A. nipponicum* 'Pictum' (also called *metallicum*) (Japanese Painted Fern) 45cm (18in), pale greyish-pink or silvery deciduous fronds, delightfully unusual fern colouration.

Asplenium scolopendrium 'Crispum'

FERNS

Blechnum Hard or Ladder ferns

❝ *Not even another* Blechnum *would call them the most beautiful of species, but the hard ferns have a robust fascination of their own, being generally dark green, almost leathery and with the simple pinnae and tough rachis giving the fronds a ladder-like appearance. The three most common species, while sharing this overall similar appearance, differ greatly in size, and planting* Blechnum tabulare *where you intended* B. penna-marina *could lead to serious embarrassment.* ❞

Blechnum penna-marina

SHADE TOLERANCE Light to deep.
SOIL Moist, organic, acidic.
HARDINESS Very hardy, tolerating at least -20°C (-4°F), except B. tabulare, fairly hardy, tolerating -10°C (14°F).
SIZE Varies widely with species, from 15 x 30cm (6 x 12in) to 1.2m x 60cm (4ft x 24in).

RECOMMENDED VARIETIES

Blechnum penna-marina 15 x 30cm (6-12in), evergreen, creeping, carpeting habit, can almost become invasive in a small bed or trough garden; B. spicant 60 x 45cm (24 x 18in) two types of frond, one widely spreading and evergreen, the other upright, spore-bearing and deciduous; B. tabulare (also called B. chilense) 1.2m x 60cm (4ft x 24in), creeping rhizomes with clumps of bronze-green more or less deciduous fronds at intervals, a plant that should only be planted where there is room for it, but a useful species for stabilizing large areas of loose wet soil.

Cryptogramma Parsley fern

❝ *I wish that this wonderful little native deciduous British plant was more widely available, for it has a combination of features that make it invaluable for some garden situations. The common name says much about the outer fronds, which have an appearance highly reminiscent of parsley. The inner fronds, on which the spores are borne have longer stems and curl back at the margins. For well-drained spots among acidic rocks, you will find no plant is more at home.* ❞

SHADE TOLERANCE Light.
SOIL Acidic, well-drained, gritty with some organic matter.
HARDINESS Very hardy, tolerating at least -20°C (-4°F).
SIZE 15 x 10cm (6 x 4in).

RECOMMENDED VARIETIES

Only the normal species, *Cryptogramma crispa*, is available.

Cystopteris fragilis

Cystopteris Bladder fern

❝ *The unusual common name of this very pretty and dainty-looking deciduous plant comes from the pale swollen covering to the young spores. The plant has a dense, congested appearance with the fronds crowded closely together, and it belongs to that most useful group of lime-tolerant species. The individual fronds remind me particularly of the leaves of some of the common white-flowered umbellifers. One species, the North American* Cystopteris bulbifera, *bears tiny bulbils on the surface of the fronds and these provide a very useful means of multiplication.* ❞

SHADE TOLERANCE
Moderate.
SOIL Preferably alkaline, well-drained with some leaf mould or similar humus.
HARDINESS Very hardy, tolerating at least -20°C (-4°F).
SIZE Varies widely with species, see below.

RECOMMENDED VARIETIES
Cystopteris bulbifera very variable in size, normally about 15-30 x 25-30cm (6-12 x 10-12in) but may be considerably more in good conditions; *C. dickieana* 15 x 10cm (6 x 4in) a scaled-down version of the other species; *C. fragilis* 45 x 30cm (18 x 12in) very fragile plant with extremely brittle fronds and a tendency to curl up for the winter with the very first hint of frost.

Dryopteris affinis

Dryopteris

❝ *I once called* Dryopteris *one of the few boring genera of ferns; and unfortunately I did it in the presence of a notable fern expert. I had in mind the native species that are pleasant enough but are, perhaps, too reminiscent of bracken to endear themselves greatly. But my remark was made a long time ago and I have since come to know some of the fine varieties of the native* D. filix-mas, *and also some of the exotic species too. I now have them in my own garden and they give me much pleasure.* ❞

SHADE TOLERANCE
Moderate to fairly deep.
SOIL Most but preferably moist, organic, well-drained.
HARDINESS Very hardy, tolerating at least -20°C (-4°F).
SIZE Varies widely with species, see right.

RECOMMENDED VARIETIES
Dryopteris filix-mas (male fern) 1.5m x 90cm (5ft x 36in) robust, finely-divided deciduous fronds, 'Crispa Cristata' 30 x 30cm (12 x 12in) neat, low-growing habit, curled and crested fronds; *D. affinis* (also called *D. borreri*) 30-45 x 30cm (12-18 x 12cm) markedly golden-brown scaly rhizome, 'Cristata The King' 60-90 x 30-45cm (24-36 x 12-18in) beautiful arching fronds with crests on each of the pinnae, almost evergreen in mild areas; *D. dilatata* (broad buckler fern) 1.2-1.5m x 60-90cm (4-5ft x 24-36in), 'Crispa Whiteside' 60 x 15-20cm (24 x 6-8in) waved and curled edges to fronds, 'Lepidota Cristata' 60 x 15-20cm (24 x 6-8in) very finely-divided pinnules and tiny crests, almost like green lace, lovely; *D. wallichiana* 60-90 x 60cm (24-36 x 24in) deciduous, dark brown-black scaly rachis contrasts with fresh green pinnae.

FERNS

Gymnocarpium

More than one fern catalogue describes Gymnocarpium dryopteris *as the loveliest native British fern, and anyone who has seen it growing wild, through the acidic leaf litter of a woodland floor would find it hard to disagree. Its more or less triangular and delicately-divided deciduous fronds arise on tough black stalks from a mass of creeping rhizomes, and it always has a fragility of form that belies a pretty tough plant. Its close relative G. robertianum is a valuable plant for alkaline soils.*

SHADE TOLERANCE Light to deep.
SOIL Moist, organic, acidic for *G. dryopteris*, alkaline for *G. robertianum*.
HARDINESS Very hardy, tolerating at least -20°C (-4°F).
SIZE Varies with species, see left.

RECOMMENDED VARIETIES
Gymnocarpium dryopteris (oak fern) 25-30 x 15-25cm (10-12 x 6-10in), 'Plumosum' is a lower-growing form in which the pinnae are larger but closely overlap; *G. robertianum* (limestone poly-pody) 30-35 x 20cm (12-14 x 8in) with golden hairs at the stem base and a fragrance of lemon.

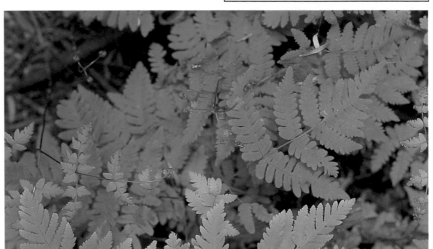

Gymnocarpium dryopteris 'Plumosum'

Matteuccia Shuttlecock fern

Not all plant names are imaginative but this one is, for the lovely erect vase-shaped clumps of fronds that arise at regular intervals from the creeping rhizomes do appear very much like tall green shuttlecocks. Its creeping capabilities shouldn't be under-estimated, however; I once planted this species at the back of a moderately-sized border and, before many seasons were out, it had not only reached the front but both sides too.

SHADE TOLERANCE Light to moderate.
SOIL Most, provided it is moist and fairly humus-rich.
HARDINESS Very hardy, toler-ating at least -20°C (-4°F).
SIZE 1m x 75-90cm (3ft x 30-36in).

RECOMMENDED VARIETIES
Normal species, *Matteuccia struthiopteris*, is usually the only one available.

Matteuccia struthiopteris

Onoclea Sensitive fern

❝ *Many plants are named because of their appearance; Onoclea sensibilis is named because of its behaviour. With the first chilling frosty nights of autumn, its fronds turn brown and die back to leave the tough, creeping rhizomes to live another day. And live they do, through the worst of winters to produce graceful, more or less triangular fronds again in spring, pinkish at first but fresh green later. It is a strongly moisture-loving plant and I have seen it used very effectively to colonize the otherwise very difficult situation of a shady stream bank.* ❞

SHADE TOLERANCE Light to moderate.
SOIL Moist, tolerant of soils that are almost waterlogged, preferably organic and slightly acid.
HARDINESS Very hardy, tolerating at least -20°C (-4°F).
SIZE 60 x 90cm (24 x 36in).

RECOMMENDED VARIETIES
Normal species, *Onoclea sensibilis,* is usually the only one available.

Onoclea sensibilis

Osmunda Royal fern

❝ *I can remember still my very first sight of Osmunda in the wild, growing at the water's edge in a wooded glade of an extensive undisturbed fen. It was obvious then, as it has been ever since, that this is, with good reason, the royal fern. Osmunda regalis is the largest British fern and a truly magnificent plant, whether seen in the wild or cultivation. Its huge deciduous fronds are simply divided and act like a huge cradle for the quite distinct, spore-bearing fronds that stand upright, as if in some fantastic dried flower arrangement. Yes, it is regal, and it is big; and should only be grown in an appropriate setting.* ❞

SHADE TOLERANCE Light to moderate.
SOIL Moist, to the point of being waterlogged, acid and organic.
HARDINESS Very hardy, tolerating at least -20°C (-4°F).
SIZE 2 x 2m (6 x 6ft) for *O. regalis.*

RECOMMENDED VARIETIES
The normal species, *Osmunda regalis,* is usually the only one available, although a rather smaller and beautiful form, *purpurascens,* is sometimes seen and is exquisite, with pinkish brown young fronds and purple stems.

Osmunda regalis

FERNS

Phegopteris Beech fern

❝ *Another species that I can describe as a 'typical' fern, in the expectation that most people will know what I mean. In the wild, the fairly finely-dissected, small, bright green deciduous fronds make an appealing carpet of growth on the floor of shady woodlands; although why it is specifically called 'beech' has always been a mystery to me, for its preference is for acid soils and it is at home with any wooded habitat that will provide this. But there's no denying the similarity between the colours of fresh beech foliage and the lovely fronds of its namesake.* ❞

SHADE TOLERANCE
Moderate to deep.
SOIL Fairly moist, organic, acidic.
HARDINESS Very hardy, tolerating at least -20°C (-4°F).
SIZE 30-45 x 30cm (12-18 x 12in).

RECOMMENDED VARIETIES
The common species, *P. connectilis*, is likely to be the only one seen.

Phegopteris connectilis

Polypodium Polypody

❝ *Even a beginner can recognise a* Polypodium, *from its appearance and, in most cases, from its habitat, too. The evergreen fronds are relatively little divided, and pretty tough too as befits a fern that can tolerate the most unlikely habitat of dry, fully-exposed limestone outcrops. It will be happy in some shade too and is lime tolerant rather than lime demanding.* ❞

SHADE TOLERANCE Light.
SOIL Most, including dry and alkaline sites, free-draining, not rich, a good fern for colonising the tops of walls.
HARDINESS Very hardy, tolerating at least -20°C (-4°F).
SIZE 30-45 x 30cm (12-18in).

RECOMMENDED VARIETIES
P. vulgare (common polypody) 'Cornubiense' best of the widely available forms with a mixture of finely- and less finely-divided fronds; *P. cambricum* 'Barrowii' broad fronds with frilled edges.

Polypodium vulgare

Polystichum Shield fern

❝ With good reason, I have a very soft spot for the genus Polystichum, as it contains my favourite of all ferns and one that crops up in various damp and shady spots in my garden. Polystichum setiferum 'Divisilobum Densum' is a really wonderful plant, but this is a big genus and has other gems too, especially in the remarkably variable species P. setiferum. The evergreen fronds are relatively large and deeply and intricately divided, even in the normal species. P. acrostichiodes is another favourite of mine. Its deep green fronds retain their colour through-out the winter. Many have a rather coarse, slightly horny feel and are perhaps better looked at rather than tampered with. ❞

RECOMMENDED VARIETIES

Polystichum setiferum (soft shield fern) 1 x 1m (3 x 3ft), 'Acutilobum' group 50-75 x 50cm (20-30 x 20in) pinnules undivided, pointed with bristles at the end, 'Congestum' group 30-50 x 30-50cm (12-20 x 12-20in) fronds tightly curled and sometimes crested, 'Divisilobum' group 1 x 1m (3 x 3ft) feathery, arching fronds, 'Divisilobum Densum' 30 x 30cm (12 x 12in) feathery fronds, overlapping to form a wonderful mound of green delight, 'Perserratum' group 45-60 x 30-45cm (18-24 x 12-18in) upright habit with finely-toothed edges to the fronds; P. tsussimense 45 x 30cm (18 x 12in) fairly com-pact dark green, upright fronds; P. polyblepharum 50 x 30cm (20 x 12in) dark green, stiff erect fronds; P. aculeatum (hard shield fern) 50-75 x 50-60cm (20-30 x 20-24in) stiff, erect, very feathery fronds, 'Gracillium' 1 x 1m (3 x 3ft) deli-cate fronds with hair-like pinnules.

SHADE TOLERANCE Light to fairly deep.
SOIL Most, including relatively dry sites, free-draining, not very rich.
HARDINESS Very hardy, tolerating at least -20°C (-4°F).
SIZE Varies widely with species, see above.

Woodsia

❝ This is one of the most delightful little deciduous ferns and could equally have appeared in a rock garden section of a book, for it is a miniature species for grow-ing in restricted space. Larger things would swamp it in a border, but it is an excellent plant for a trough garden or special fern bed. It produces rather slender, dark green, but perfectly scaled-down and typically divided fronds. I always plant it peeping out from beneath a large rock or, I think even prettier, an old log. ❞

SHADE TOLERANCE Light to moderate.
SOIL Free-draining, preferably at least slightly acidic, not very rich.
HARDINESS Very hardy, toler-ating at least -20°C (-4°F).
SIZE 10 x 10cm (4 x 4in).

RECOMMENDED VARIETIES
There are several rather similar species, none as widely available as I would wish, so choose whatever is on offer. Woodsia intermedia is perhaps the commonest.

Polystichum setiferum

ANNUALS

True annuals are plants that take less than one year to pass from seed to flower and seed again. Clearly, therefore, they grow quickly, their metabolism is fast and there is relatively little room for stress or strain in their lives. For green plants to grow quickly, they must have access to high light levels in order for photosynthesis to proceed apace and, for this reason, annuals occur relatively infrequently in shady environments. If this is true of natural habitats, it's true of gardens too and so the annual is a rarity in the shade garden. It's worth adding that many of the plants that we grow as garden annuals are, in reality, tender perennials but the reasoning behind their need to grow quickly from seed and thus their general unreliability in shade still holds true.

This creates problems for the gardener wanting bright and fairly quick colour in a shady place, and there are only two effective solutions. The first is to restrict planting to the few species that are moderately shade tolerant and to make full use of the range of varieties in which they exist. The second is to use annuals that are intolerant of shade but to grow them in containers so they can be moved in and out of shaded areas; perhaps one week in shade followed by two weeks in the sun to recover. The latter approach can be applied to almost all familiar summer annuals and falls outside the scope of this book, but the following accounts are of the six types of annual that I have found most successful when kept constantly in light to moderate shade; no annuals will thrive in deep shade.

RAISING ANNUALS FOR THE SHADE GARDEN

Although two of my selected annuals are hardy, I find that raising all of them by the half-hardy annual technique in the greenhouse, and then putting them out as young plants, works best. Expecting not only that plants will

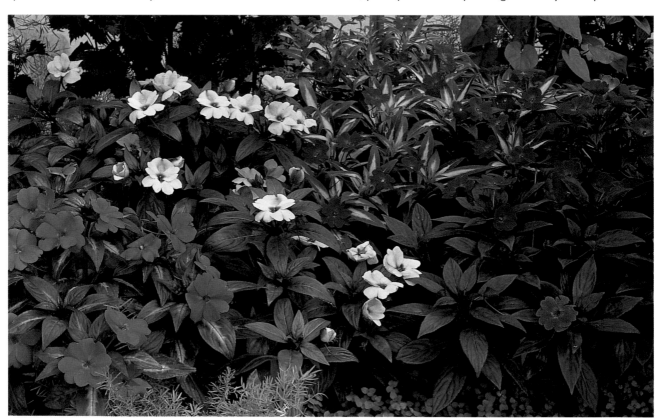

Impatiens 'New Guinea Hybrids' make a delightfully colourful addition to the border

grow in shade but that their seeds should germinate rapidly and reliably in shaded conditions, too, is asking rather too much of them. I now use a soil-based seedling compost, such as John Innes, for all annuals, but lighten it by adding one-quarter by volume of sand. Some form of propagator and some additional heat are needed. The best and least expensive way of supplying these is with a seed-tray-style propagator with a rigid but ventilated plastic cover placed on a heated propagation bench (a sand bench) or heating mat in the greenhouse.

Prick on seedlings when they are large enough to handle, but this task can be eliminated if the seeds are sown individually or in small batches into modular inserts in the seed trays. All plants should be hardened-off before being put out when the danger of the last frost has passed. Clearly, all of this effort can be dispensed with if you buy young plants rather than raising them yourself (although even then, they will benefit from a week or 10 days of hardening-off), but you will not have access to the full range of varieties. For most gardeners, a practical compromise is to buy the commoner varieties as plants, and to raise yourself those that garden centres and nurseries don't stock routinely.

PLANTING AND CARE

The soil should be prepared in advance by being thoroughly dug and, if it is heavy and clayey, lightened with organic matter. The closer to planting time that the soil is dug, the more rotted and friable should be the organic matter used. On very heavy soils, it is sensible to raise the soil bed slightly to improve drainage. Rake in a general

A cheerful combination of *Nicotiana* and *Lobelia*

fertilizer, roughly 29g per 0.84 sq m (1oz per sq yd) about two weeks before planting.

As with almost all herbaceous plants, annuals will give the most effective display if they are planted in small groups, rather than in vast masses, or as odd ones. They will establish best if 'watered in' with a liquid fertilizer rather than with water and then given liquid fertilizer about once every two weeks. They should not be allowed to dry out but nor should they be allowed to become waterlogged – no annuals thrive in wet, heavy or cold soils. Although it is scarcely practical with very small-flowered plants such as lobelias, those annuals with larger

blooms should be routinely deadheaded. Not only will this improve their appearance and stimulate new flowers to form, but it will also lessen the chances of grey mould which can be a problem in damp, shady positions.

Apart from grey mould, annuals are relatively free from pests and diseases although in a shaded situation, there may be problems from mildew and from pests such as woodlice and aphids. Combat mildew with a proprietary systemic fungicide or with sulphur, while woodlice and other chewing pests, as well as aphids, can be controlled with a spray or powder formulation of a contact insecticide such as permethrin or derris.

ANNUALS

Begonia

❝ Annual begonias are derived from crosses between two South American species, and are generally called Begonia semperflorens. *They are not, under any circumstances, to be compared with the large-flowered tuberous and non-stop begonias in colours more reminiscent of something medical than horticultural. The lush, glossy and almost succulent foliage is appealing in its own right, but also provides the perfect foil for the flowers. The range of flower colour is from bright, striking green to a more classic bronze. ❞*

SEED SOWING On the compost surface in very small groups.
GERMINATION TEMPERATURE 21-25°C (70-77°F).
APPROXIMATE TIME NEEDED FROM SOWING TO PLANTING OUT
17 weeks.
SPACING BETWEEN PLANTS 15cm (6in).
SIZE Differs slightly with variety, but averages 10-15 x 10cm (4-6 x 4in).
HARDINESS/TRUE STATUS
Barely-hardy perennial, tolerating no less than 0°C (32°F).
RELIABILITY IN SHADE
Very good.

RECOMMENDED VARIETIES
The blend of leaf and flower colour that you obtain depends upon the mixtures that have been compiled by individual seed companies, so there is little merit in listing specific names, but do read the catalogue or packet descriptions carefully if you want particular combinations. Pure white flowers on plants with green foliage are especially striking in the shade, and this combination is usually called 'Olympia White'. Any variety prefixed with 'Verdo' will also have green leaves, while any prefixed 'Coco' will have bronze leaves. There are red, pink and white flowered forms in both ranges.

Begonia semperflorens

Collinsia

❝ I must admit, if I am honest, that collinsias wouldn't merit much interest if they weren't shade tolerant, for there are similar but better plants for the open garden. Nonetheless, these members of the Leguminosae, *derived from the Californian* Collinsia bicolor *do have an individual appeal with their characteristically lipped flowers, typically white in the upper part and purple in the lower. At one time, pure white and pure purples were available, but I haven't seen these for many years. ❞*

SEED SOWING 0.5cm (¼in) deep, individually.
GERMINATION TEMPERATURE 15-20°C (60-68°F).
APPROXIMATE TIME NEEDED FROM SOWING TO PLANTING OUT
8 weeks.
SPACING BETWEEN PLANTS 20-25cm (8-10in).
SIZE 60 x 15-20cm (24 x 6-8in).
HARDINESS/TRUE STATUS
Barely-hardy annual, tolerating -5°C (23°F).
RELIABILITY IN SHADE
Good.

RECOMMENDED VARIETIES
Because the old single colours seem to have vanished, you will only be able to obtain plants that are selections of the true species, sometimes sold under the name 'Innocent' or 'Innocence'.

Impatiens

&6 Love them or not, you can't ignore Impatiens walleriana, *for it is from this East African species that the bedding busy lizzie has been derived and has risen to such a prominent position in recent years. The modern varieties offer an astonishingly floriferous habit on neat, compact plants, with a long flowering season, a wide range of colours from white through pinks and reds to vibrant orange, and a better tolerance of shade than any other annual. Over the past few seasons, they have been joined by plants that, to my mind, are even better, the so-called 'New Guinea Hybrids', developed from* I. hawkeri *from New Guinea and adjoining areas. These have similar flowers, although not in such a wide range of colours, but also the enormous additional merit of very attractive foliage in shades of green, red and bronze with some stunning variegations. Although now widely available as plants, increasing numbers of New Guinea hybrids will be offered for raising from seed. 99*

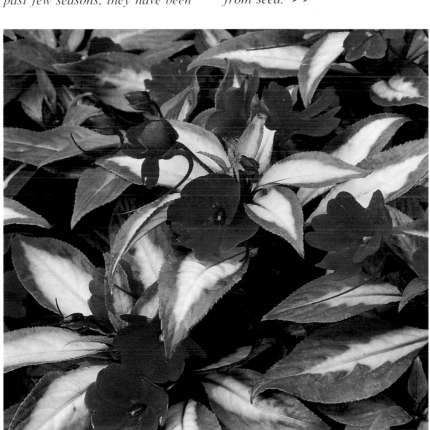

Impatiens **'New Guinea Hybrid'**

SEED SOWING On the compost surface in very small groups.
GERMINATION TEMPERATURE 21-24°C (70-75°F); this is critical.
APPROXIMATE TIME NEEDED FROM SOWING TO PLANTING OUT 16-17 weeks.
SPACING BETWEEN PLANTS 15cm (6in).
SIZE Differs with variety, from 10 x 10cm (4 x 4in) for 'Novette', to 30 x 20cm (12 x 8in) for 'Mega Orange Star'.
HARDINESS/TRUE STATUS Barely-hardy perennial, tolerating no less than 0°C (32°F).
RELIABILITY IN SHADE Very good.

RECOMMENDED VARIETIES
The range of busy lizzies is so big as to be bewildering, and every seed company has a large number of its own selections and mixtures. They are generally subdivided into a number of main groups, however, and it is these that are most simply understood: Multiflora types, very large numbers of fairly big single flowers on compact plants, including 'Accent', 'Novette' and 'Super Elfin' strains; 'Blitz' series, very large single flowers, available as separate colours or as mixtures; 'Doubles', although all so-called double mixtures will include some single and semi-double flowered plants. Additionally, there are the 'New Guinea Hybrids' with their large flowers and attractive foliage patterns.

ANNUALS

Lobelia

" *Lobelias are among the mainstays of my summer-flowering annuals and I find their lovely masses of blue flowers ideal for use in hanging baskets, for edging and particularly for containers, in all parts of the garden. The familiar bedding types are derived from the South African* Lobelia erinus *but you won't very often find them recommended for use in shade. They have, however, performed reasonably well for me and, as there are no other plants of this colour and habit for shady places, they are well worth trying.* "

SEED SOWING On the compost surface in very small groups.
GERMINATION TEMPERATURE 20-25°C (68-77°F).
APPROXIMATE TIME NEEDED FROM SOWING TO PLANTING OUT 14 weeks.
SPACING BETWEEN PLANTS 10-15cm (4-6in).
SIZE Differs with variety from about 15 x 15cm (6 x 6in).
HARDINESS/TRUE STATUS Barely-hardy perennial, tolerating no less than 0°C (32°F).
RELIABILITY IN SHADE Moderate.

RECOMMENDED VARIETIES
Over the years, various selections of white lobelia have appeared, but none are really reliable in the sense that all include some blue-flowered plants and none are really compact. Reddish varieties are available, too, but the real merit of the bedding lobelia is its blue flowers. I try all of the new variants, but come back constantly to the dark blue 'Crystal Palace' with its bronze-green foliage, the blue flowers and white eye of 'Mrs Clibran', and the pale blue of 'Cambridge Blue'. For a hanging basket in the shade, then choose one of the 'Cascade' range.

Nemophila

" *Nemophilas are sometimes called Californian bluebells which is, I suppose, fair enough since they come from western North America and have more or less blue bell-shaped flowers. In reality, I find them oddities for, unlike most plants from warm climates, they fare better in cool damp summers and in cool shady places than they do in full sun – they are not just shade tolerant, they are shade demanding. The flowers are also borne atop feeble, fern-leaved stems that benefit from some light wrap-around or twiggy support. But, of course, all of this adds up to an extremely valuable shade-garden annual, and one that must surely increase in popularity.* "

SEED SOWING 0.5cm (¼in) deep, individually.
GERMINATION TEMPERATURE 15-20°C (60-68°F).
APPROXIMATE TIME NEEDED FROM SOWING TO PLANTING OUT 8 weeks.

SPACING BETWEEN PLANTS 15cm (6in).
SIZE Differs with variety, from 15-20 x 10cm (6-8 x 4in).
HARDINESS/TRUE STATUS Barely-hardy annual, tolerating no less than 0°C (32°F).
RELIABILITY IN SHADE Good.

Nemophila maculata

RECOMMENDED VARIETIES
Two species are behind the garden varieties: *Nemophila maculata*, sometimes called 'Five Spot', which has rather remarkable single flowers, each with five white petals bearing a small dark purple blotch at the tip; and *N. menziesii* (sometimes called *N. insignis*) or 'Baby Blue Eyes' typically with clear blue, white-centred flowers although, at one time, colour variants were available, too.

Nicotiana

❝ *It doesn't need a deep knowledge of language to work out that* Nicotiana *is the genus that includes the tobacco plant, and you will probably find these richly-scented plants listed in seed catalogues as ornamental tobacco. It is the perfume that is their real virtue, although the range of flower colours available has been extended in recent years to include white, greenish-yellows, pinks and red. Various tropical species have been used to develop the garden varieties and these are commonly listed in catalogues, the variation coming mainly from intensity of perfume, number and size of flowers. They are all, however, the biggest of the shade-tolerant annuals.* ❞

SEED SOWING On the compost surface in very small groups.
GERMINATION TEMPERATURE 15-20°C (60-68°F).
APPROXIMATE TIME NEEDED FROM SOWING TO PLANTING OUT 10 weeks.
SPACING BETWEEN PLANTS 30cm (12in).
SIZE Differs with variety, from about 30 x 10cm (12 x 4in) for 'Domino' series, to 1.2m x 30cm (4ft x 12in) for *N. langsdorffii*.
HARDINESS/TRUE STATUS Barely/fairly hardy perennial, tolerating -5°C (23°F) or slightly less.
RELIABILITY IN SHADE Moderate.

RECOMMENDED VARIETIES

Nicotiana alata strong perfume, erect branches and mid-green coloured leaves, wide colour range in mixtures of medium-sized flowers, 'Sensation Mixed' is a popular mixture but the 'Domino' range offers both mixtures as well as individual flower colours, 'Domino White' is a particularly good shade-garden plant. Others of this general type are included in the 'Nicky' range. *N. langsdorfii* is a tall plant with interesting, elongated lime-green flowers.

Nicotiana from the 'Domino' range

GRASSES AND GRASS-LIKE PLANTS

Gardeners often ask me how they can manage to create a lawn beneath trees or in some other shaded spot. My usual response is to suggest that they take a walk to the nearest area of natural or semi-natural woodland and look downwards. Having done so, they will never see anything that resembles a lawn, even an unmown one and, indeed, they will see relatively little grass of any type. For the types of grass that tolerate being mown will not tolerate shade (which is why there is no account of lawns in this book) and, indeed, the types of grass that will tolerate any sort of shade are fairly limited.

Nonetheless, the few grass species that do occur in natural woodland tend to be very attractive ones. Over the past few years, the importance of ornamental grasses (beyond lawns) has come to be recognized in gardens, so their value in the shade garden should also be appreciated. With few exceptions (none of which are included here), I don't advise raising ornamental grasses from seed, for the best forms do not usually come true, and it is, therefore preferable to buy plants of named selections or varieties from a reputable nursery. They should be planted in exactly the same way as other herbaceous perennials (p. 68). In general, they require similar care both after planting and also when established, but have the singular merit of needing no staking. Dead seedheads are as attractive as living ones and, in most cases, are best left overwinter to then be cut back and generally tidied up in spring. Grasses and grass-like plants (in which I also include sedges and rushes) may be divided in either the spring or the autumn in the usual way. There are grasses, sedges and rushes adapted to almost all types of habitat and soil, and this is true of the shade tolerant species, too.

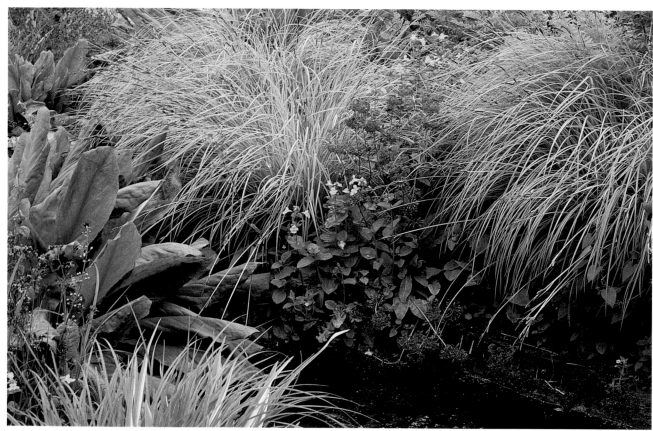

The narrow grass-like foliage of *Carex morrowii* makes an impressive display beside a garden pool

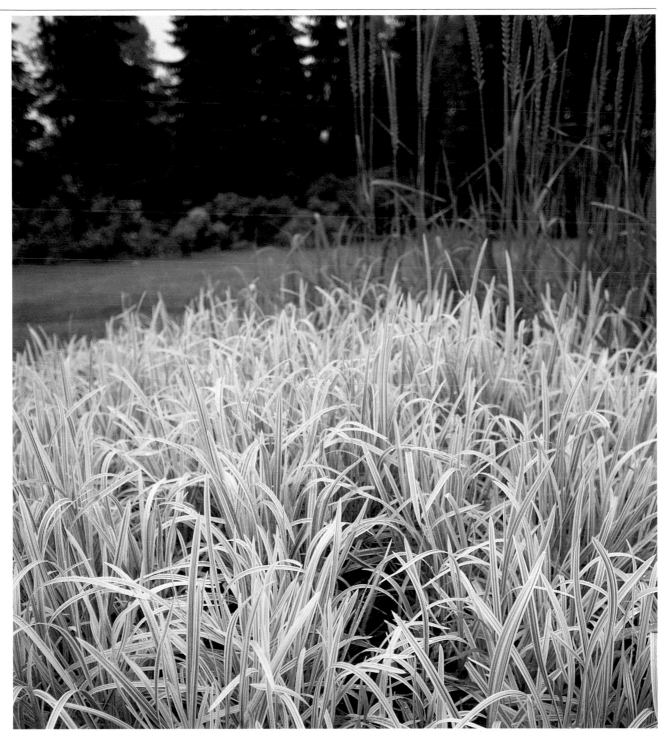

Ornamental grasses make an attractive addition to the shady garden

GRASSES AND GRASS-LIKE PLANTS

Carex morrowii 'Evergold'

Carex Sedges

❝ *Years ago, I used to be entranced by finding the native pendulous sedge in its natural habitat in limestone woods. It helped to create my long-standing affection for sedges in general, and I have since enjoyed the company of several of them in the wooded parts of my own garden. Carex is the largest genus in the sedge family, their leaves typically differing from grasses in being keeled or V-shaped in cross-section. They also tend to feel tougher and coarser than most grasses and are more frequently found in damp places. Sedge flowers are generally more robust, attractively so and, although the natural species are pleasing enough, there are also some most attractive forms with variegated foliage.* ❞

SHADE TOLERANCE Light to moderate, preferably dappled.
SOIL Moist, preferably organic, not very rich.
HARDINESS Very hardy, tolerating at least -20°C (-4°F).
SIZE Varies with species, see right.

RECOMMENDED VARIETIES

There are numerous species and many varieties, most of which, except perhaps the very brightly-variegated types, are worth trying in shade but the following I can vouch for: *Carex buchananii* (leather leaf sedge) 60 x 20cm (24 x 8in) slender, reddish-bronze foliage; *C. comans* 50 x 50cm (20 x 20in) neat, compact mound of slender brownish foliage; *C. morrowii* 'Variegata' 35 x 25cm (14 x 10in) rough to touch, leaves margined and streaked white, flowers rarely; *C. pendula* 1.2m x 60cm (4ft x 24in) beautiful arching habit with drooping flower heads.

Luzula Woodrush

❝ *Rushes differ from grasses in that their leaves have a rounded appearance in cross-section. Not many species are important as garden ornamentals although a few, especially those in the woodrush genus,* Luzula, *can be significant lawn weeds on impoverished soils. Nonetheless, I feel that even they fall into the category of those plants that, were they not weeds, would be appreciated as rather attractive little things. They are the converse of the sedges in generally* preferring drier soils, and so the woodland species join that small but valuable group of plants for situations in dry shade. ❞

SHADE TOLERANCE Light to moderate, preferably dappled.
SOIL Fairly dry, sandy, not very rich.
HARDINESS Very hardy, tolerating at least -20°C (-4°F).
SIZE 45 x 45cm (18 x 18in) for *L. nivea*, 30 x 30cm (12 x 12in) for *L. sylvatica*.

RECOMMENDED VARIETIES

Luzula nivea (snowy woodrush) beautiful massed heads of white flowers, a lovely plant for the dry woodland edge; *L. sylvatica* (greater woodrush) fresh, bright green leaves, unusual for a woodrush, with greenish flowers (p.121).

Deschampsia flexuosa

Deschampsia Hair grass

❝ *The name 'hair grass' says it all, for the deschampsias have narrow, graceful foliage arising from a neat tussock and producing the most delightful shimmering flower spikes. For me, they are among the most characteristic grasses of woodland glades and look especially endearing as the shafts of early sunlight catch them on a summer's morning. They are easy, undemanding, and with only the slightest tendency to misbehave and self-seed.* ❞

SHADE TOLERANCE Light, dappled.
SOIL Most except very dry and impoverished; fairly rich, slightly organic soils preferred.
HARDINESS Very hardy, tolerating at least -20°C (-4°F).
SIZE 1 x 1m (3 x 3ft) for *D. caespitosa* and cultivars, 70 x 70cm (28 x 28in) for *D. flexuosa*.

RECOMMENDED VARIETIES

Deschampsia caespitosa (tufted hair grass) the normal species is pretty enough but the selected forms are even better: 'Bronzeschleier' ('Bronze Veil') particularly fine bronze foliage and flower spikes, 'Goldschleier' ('Golden Veil') flower stems and foliage initially green, then turning yellowish-gold; *D. flexuosa* smaller in overall form and possibly slightly more shade tolerant.

GRASSES AND GRASS-LIKE PLANTS

Hakonechloa

❝*In a relatively short time, one grass has probably endeared itself more to gardeners' affections than any other; and this despite being deciduous and having one of the most tongue-twisting of names.* Hakonechloa macra *is a fairly low-growing Japanese species, with soft, broad leaves and, in its selected forms, the most beautiful golden stripes. In common with most variegated plants, it will not tolerate serious shade but at the edge of a shade border, it is an absolute delight, especially if it is planted close to a blue-flowered plant which it can embrace.* ❞

SHADE TOLERANCE Light, dappled.
SOIL Tolerates most, provided it is not very wet or very dry.
HARDINESS Very hardy, tolerating at least -20°C (-4°F).
SIZE 25 x 40cm (10 x 16in).

RECOMMENDED VARIETIES
There are two commonly-available forms: *Hakonechloa macra* 'Alboaurea' with yellow and white variegation, and 'Aureola' with vivid golden-yellow leaves and only a few narrow stripes of green. Both are lovely.

Holcus Soft grass

❝*You can't really have a simpler or more descriptive name than soft grass, and it sums up perfectly this lovely mat-forming plant for woodland glades. But what a Jekyll and Hyde species it is, for the normal species is an aggressive and invasive weed, second only to couch in its nuisance value. By contrast, the variegated form is almost as docile as a lamb and can safely be given a home, with virtual impunity, in any shady border.* ❞

SHADE TOLERANCE Light, dappled.
SOIL Tolerates most, provided it is not very wet or very dry.
HARDINESS Very hardy, tolerating at least -20°C (-4°F).
SIZE 30 x 50cm (12 x 20in).

RECOMMENDED VARIETIES
The variety, the *only* variety to grow is the variegated *Holcus mollis* 'Albovariegatus' which has leaves with white margins.

Hakonechloa macra 'Aureola'

Holcus mollis 'Albovariegatus'

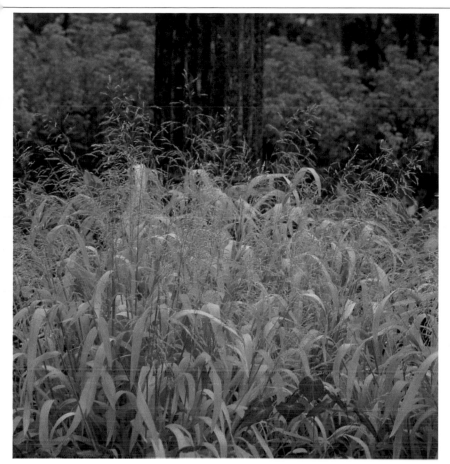

Milium effusum 'Aureum'

Milium Wood millet

❝ *A genuine clump-forming grass but grown as an ornamental only in its golden-foliaged form. I interplant it with woodland bulbs which it complements perfectly, its only drawback being a tendency to be short-lived. Even this is countered by it coming true from seed and so if you are lucky it will perpetuate itself without more effort. The foliage, even in the golden variant is still green but with an almost intangible golden flush.* ❞

SHADE TOLERANCE Light, dappled.
SOIL Tolerates most, provided it is not very wet or very dry.
HARDINESS Very hardy, tolerating at least -20°C (-4°F).
SIZE 45 x 30cm (18 x 12in).

RECOMMENDED VARIETIES
The golden-leaved variant of *Milium effusum* is usually called 'Bowles' Golden Grass'.

Molinia Moor grass

❝ *Moorland tends to be wet, and so logic suggests that the moor grass requires damp soils. Moors are also acidic, and so it also needs a naturally peaty site. If you can satisfy these conditions, then this plant will truly be at home but, in practice, it is more widely tolerant and will thrive in most gardens that are not very dry or alkaline. Although popularly called 'purple' moor grass, and when seen en masse, there is indeed a purple haze, the autumn colour on close inspection will be seen to change from green to brown rather than true purple. It is a fairly neat, tufted plant and, as in nature, really looks better, I always feel, when planted in drifts rather than as isolated specimens.* ❞

SHADE TOLERANCE Light to moderate, preferably dappled.
SOIL Tolerates most, but best on moist, organic, acid soils.
HARDINESS Very hardy, tolerating at least -20°C (-4°F).
SIZE 50 x 50cm (20 x 20in).

RECOMMENDED VARIETIES
Molinia caerulea is the normal species, of which there are several variants with German names but differing mainly in the height and arching nature of the flower stalks. The best named variant is one with white-striped leaves called 'Variegata'.

INDEX

PHOTOGRAPHIC ACKNOWLEDGEMENTS

The Publisher would like to thank the following for their kind permission to reproduce the photographs in this book:

Front cover: John Glover

Dr. Stefan Buczacki 14, 16 left, 71 left; Eric Crichton 8, 21, 31 right, 41, 43 bottom right, 44, 46, 48 top, 49 bottom, 56, 68, 77 top, 81, 91 right, 94, 100 top right, 102 top and bottom, 113, 118, 120; John Fielding 6, 16 right, 71 right; John Glover 7, 22, 24, 26, 27 top left, 51 top right and bottom left, 53, 55, 65, 86, 89, 103, 111, 114; Derek Gould 10, 25 bottom left and bottom right, 38, 39, 43, 59, 78, 88, 101, 122, 124 bottom left, 125 bottom right; Photos Horticultural 11, 13, 27 bottom right, 28, 30, 32, 33 top left, 36, 40, 42, 45 top, 48 bottom, 54, 57, 58, 60, 61, 62, 63, 69 bottom right, 73, 76, 82, 83 top left and bottom right, 84 bottom right, 85 bottom, 87, 89 left, 91 left, 93 top and bottom, 96, 97, 99, 100 bottom left, 108 bottom left and bottom right, 109 bottom right, 110 bottom left, 112 top, 115, 116, 119, 123, 124 bottom right; Andrew Lawson 9, 50, 72, 74, 90, 104, 117; S & O Mathews 23, 29, 31 left, 66, 69 left, 70, 77 bottom, 107 bottom left, 111 bottom left; Harry Smith Collection 3, 12, 18 top and bottom right, 19 bottom right, 20, 33 right, 34, 35, 37, 45 bottom, 47, 52, 64, 67, 75, 79, 80, 85 top, 92, 95, 98, 106, 107 top right, 110 right, 112 bottom, 121.

TEMPERATURE CHART		
BARELY HARDY	0 to -5°C	32 to 23°F
FAIRLY HARDY	-5 to -10°C	23 to 14°F
MODERATELY HARDY	-10 to -15°C	14 to 5°F
HARDY	-15 to -20°C	5 to -4°F
VERY HARDY	-20°C or below	-4°F or below